Praise for *The Long Way Here*

"*The Long Way Here* is a powerfully personal story of growth, hope, and the journey to finding peace and purpose. Anne Spoldi creates a space for readers to find perspective on their lives, evaluate priorities, and realign with what really matters to them. It's a chance to create a renewed sense of purpose with clarity and compassion for yourself. Read it and reflect—it will transform your life."

—**Dr. Marshall Goldsmith,** Thinkers50 #1 Executive Coach and *New York Times* bestselling author of *The Earned Life, Triggers,* and *What Got You Here Won't Get You There*

"Anne Spoldi's *The Long Way Here* is a powerful reminder that real leadership starts with integrity and self-awareness. Anne brings honesty, heart, and hard-earned lessons to every story. I saw those qualities in her at Sun Microsystems, and it's great to see her paying it forward—helping others lead with purpose and authenticity."

—**Scott McNealy,** Co-Founder and Former CEO, Sun Microsystems

"Anne Spoldi has always had a rare gift for transforming not just organizations but the people within them. *The Long Way Here* captures that same spirit—inviting readers to embrace change, courage, and authenticity with grace. Her stories remind us that leadership begins with heart and grows through reflection and resilience. I've seen firsthand how Anne inspires lasting transformation wherever she leads, and this book is a beautiful extension of that gift. A must-read for anyone committed to leading with purpose and humanity."

—**Clark Golestani,** Private Equity and Venture Capital Investor, Board Director

THE
LONG
WAY
HERE

THE
LONG
WAY
HERE

STORIES THAT INSPIRE
Resilience, Growth, and
the Courage to Lead

ANNE SPOLDI

PROSSIMO
PRESS

The Long Way Here
Stories That Inspire Resilience, Growth, and the Courage to Lead

Copyright 2025 © Anne Spoldi

PROSSIMO
P R E S S

Published by Prossimo Press
Gladstone, NJ

Edited by Tracy Rothschild Lynch, Bluebird Editorial
Cover design and typesetting by G Sharp Design, LLC

First edition, November 2025

Paperback ISBN: 979-8-9932524-0-7
Ebook ISBN: 979-8-9932524-1-4

Created in the United States of America

With deep love and gratitude, I dedicate this book to my amazing, smart, kind, and thoughtful daughter, Emma. She is determined. Bold. And dedicated to whatever she focuses on. The countless lessons I've learned from her have made me who I am today. Every time I hear Emma say "Mama," it reaches a special place in my heart I once believed would stay empty forever. The story of how you came into my life lives in these pages.

I also want to pay tribute to all my coaching clients over the years. Each of you holds a special place in my heart, and I have learned so much from your dedication to personal and professional development. Your commitment has inspired me to become the best coach I can be.

And finally, I dedicate this book to every woman who has chosen to rise, even when it would have been easier to stay low, stay silent.

Your voice matters.

Your leadership matters.

Your story matters.

Courage starts with showing up
and letting ourselves be seen.

— BRENÉ BROWN

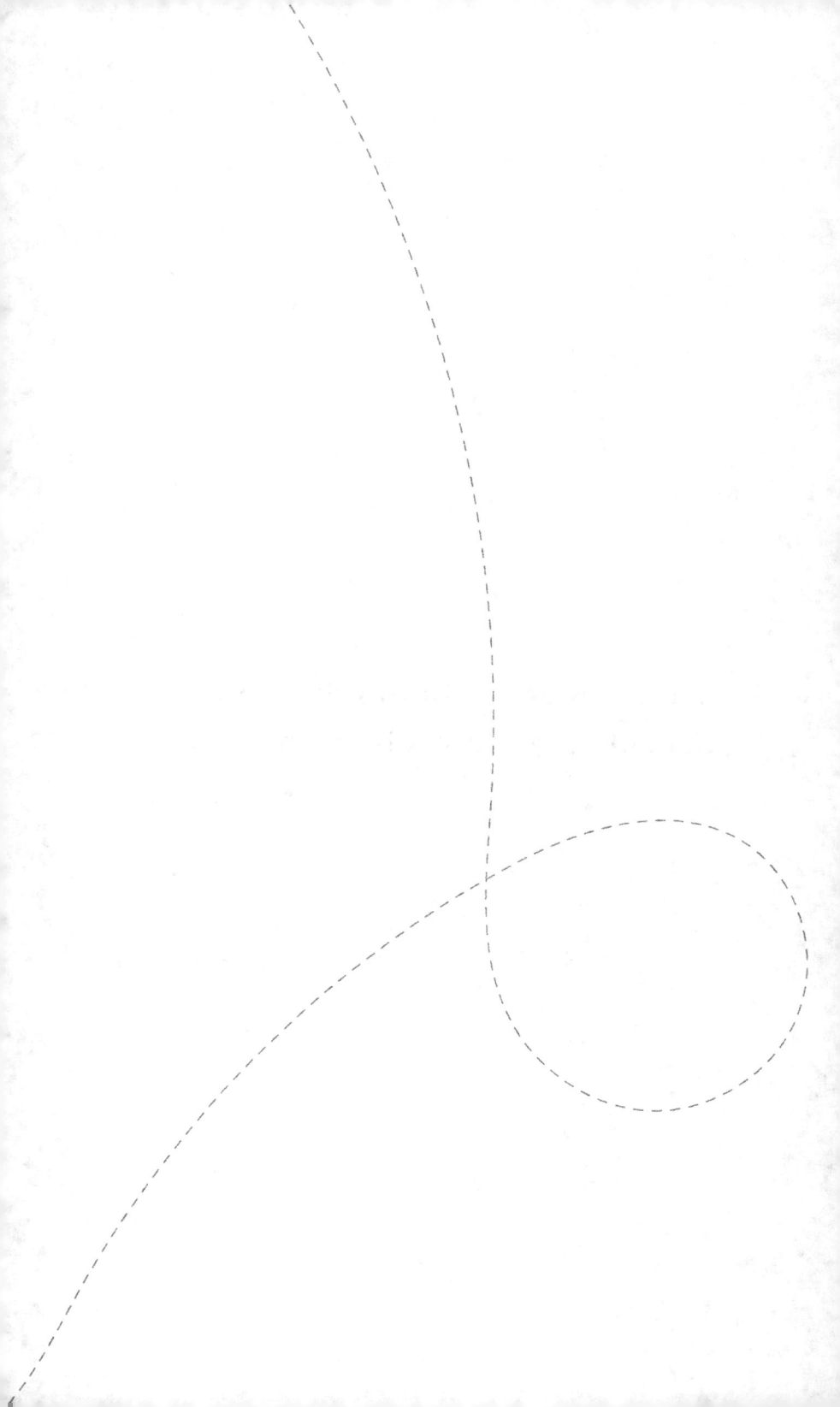

CONTENTS

PART III: OWNING YOUR LEADERSHIP JOURNEY

PART IV: LEADERSHIP FROM THE INSIDE OUT

PART V: THE GROWTH EDGE

PART VI: CONTINUING THE JOURNEY

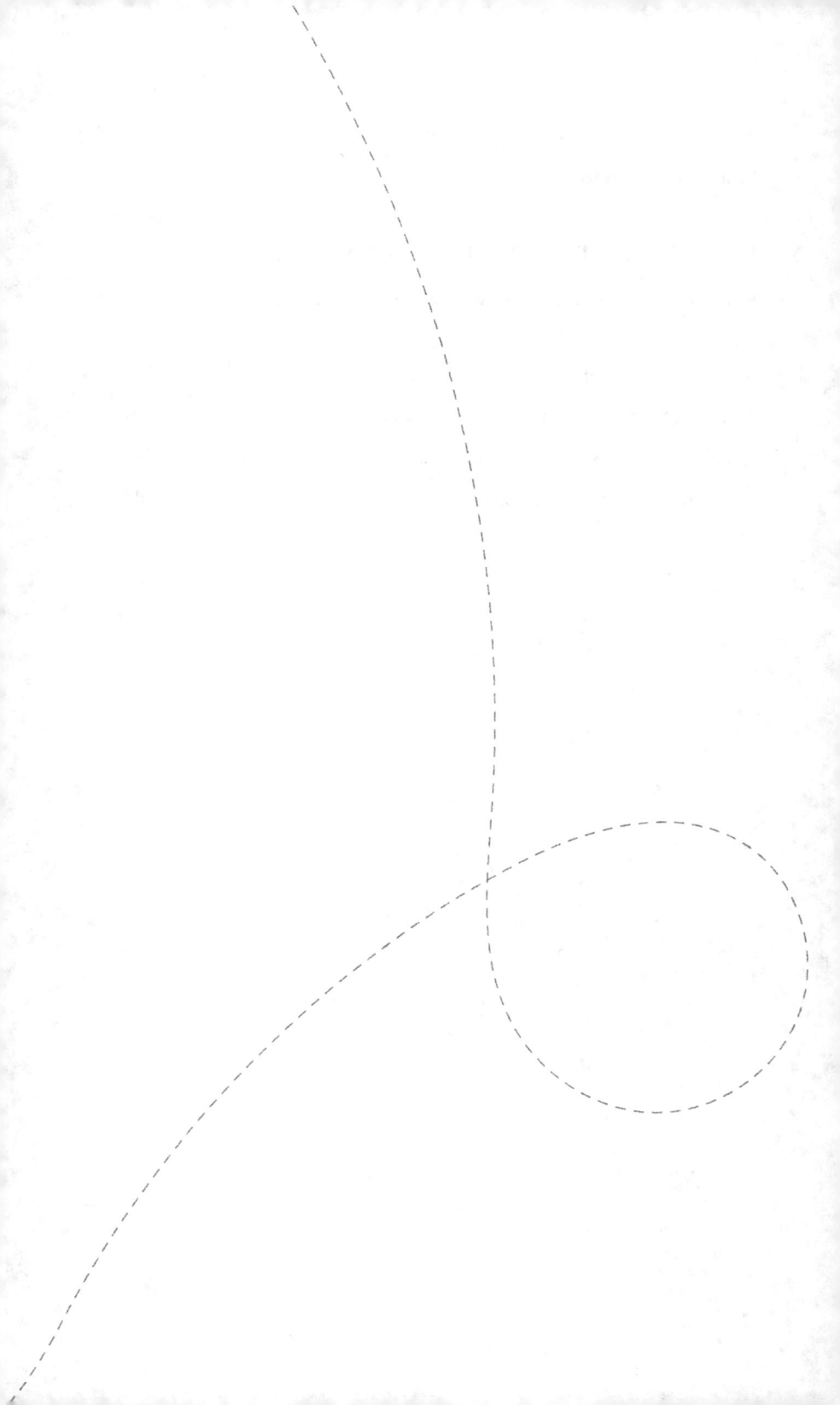

INTRODUCTION

LEADERSHIP ISN'T JUST about titles, promotions, or the proverbial corner offices. It's not reserved for executives or those in charge. Leadership begins within—in how we make choices, demonstrate care for others, and carry ourselves through the world. The first person any of us leads is ourselves.

In my work as a leadership coach, I've come to believe that leadership is less about what we do and more about how we do it. Leadership is woven into our everyday actions—how we listen, how we show up for others, and how we navigate challenge and change. It's as relevant in a corporate boardroom as it is around a family dinner table, at a PTA meeting, in a hospital ward, or on the sidelines of a soccer field.

This book is for emerging leaders. It's for the women stepping into leadership—not just in formal roles but in all the ways they're learning to trust their voice, stand in their values, and lead with authenticity. It's also for the mentors, coaches, and champions who help them see what's possible—sometimes before they can see it themselves. I've been pleasantly surprised to discover that several of my male colleagues and clients, whom I invited to be early readers of the manuscript, also deeply connected with its message. Their responses reminded me that the insights shared within these pages can invite all readers to explore the beauty of collaboration, growth, and the shared journey of effective leadership.

When I became a leadership coach, I felt blessed knowing that I was following my passion to have an impact on more people in the world. What I didn't know was that the people I coached would in turn coach and teach others what they learned from our conversations. I have been further blessed to realize that by being a coach, I have increased my "net effect" exponentially.

I then revisited my goal and allowed myself to wonder what once seemed impossible: Can I extend my reach beyond the scope and ripple effect of my clients by writing a book? By helping people I've never met? I was up for the challenge, for sure, but then I was faced with an important question: How?

I decided ultimately to go with what I know: my own experience. Within these pages, I offer thirty-six stories that call upon my own experience as a woman, a daughter, a student, a mother, a colleague, an executive, and—now—a professional coach. Through real stories of growth, vulnerability, and hope, I've written with my past in mind in order to offer encouragement and inspiration to the futures of my readers. The order of the stories is organic—their connection lives in threads and memories I've revisited often throughout my life and my time as a leadership coach.

My intention in sharing my stories is simple: to offer encouragement and inspiration to anyone who has ever doubted their voice or their path. At the end of each story (except one), I've provided journaling exercises to encourage your own self-reflection, because I truly believe this is where true growth begins. Each chapter concludes with a gentle reminder—a little sticky note from me to you, to remember the essence of the story in the simplest of formats as you set forth on the next step of your journey.

As you read, I invite you to remember what I consider the most important lesson of all: True leadership doesn't begin with perfection—but with heart.

WHEN JOURNALING
IN THIS BOOK

AS A LEADERSHIP coach, I ask every client to keep a journal. Why? Because growth begins with reflection. Whether you're navigating a career decision, building confidence, or simply noticing more about how you show up in the world, journaling creates space and time for insight—the kind of insight that doesn't always come in the moment but reveals itself when you pause long enough to listen.

If you're new to journaling, don't worry—there's no one "right" way to do it. You don't need to fill multiple pages or craft perfect sentences. In fact, some of the most powerful entries are simply a word, a phrase, or a single sentence that captures how something specific "landed" for you. You might jot down an emotion, a question, a shift in perspective, or even a sketch. You may reflect on something a coworker said or imagine how a situation could play out. It's about reflection, not overthinking. What matters most is taking time to be with your own thoughts—and to notice what calls to you.

In this book, each story ends with one or more journaling prompts. Consider these an invitation to pause, reflect, and engage with your own related experiences. I recommend using a special journal just for this book. Many of my clients handwrite their responses because there's something about pen to paper that grounds them. The pen-to-paper technique may, in fact, slow you down and help you connect more deeply with what you're feeling and discovering as internal thoughts become external reflections. For others, crafting on a keyboard accomplishes the same thing.

Journaling is a practice, not a performance. Think of it as a private space where your inner voice can speak freely. Let go of expectations. Let it be imperfect. Let it be yours.

Whether you fill pages or just capture a sentence or two, you're creating a path to self-awareness—and that's where real transformation begins.

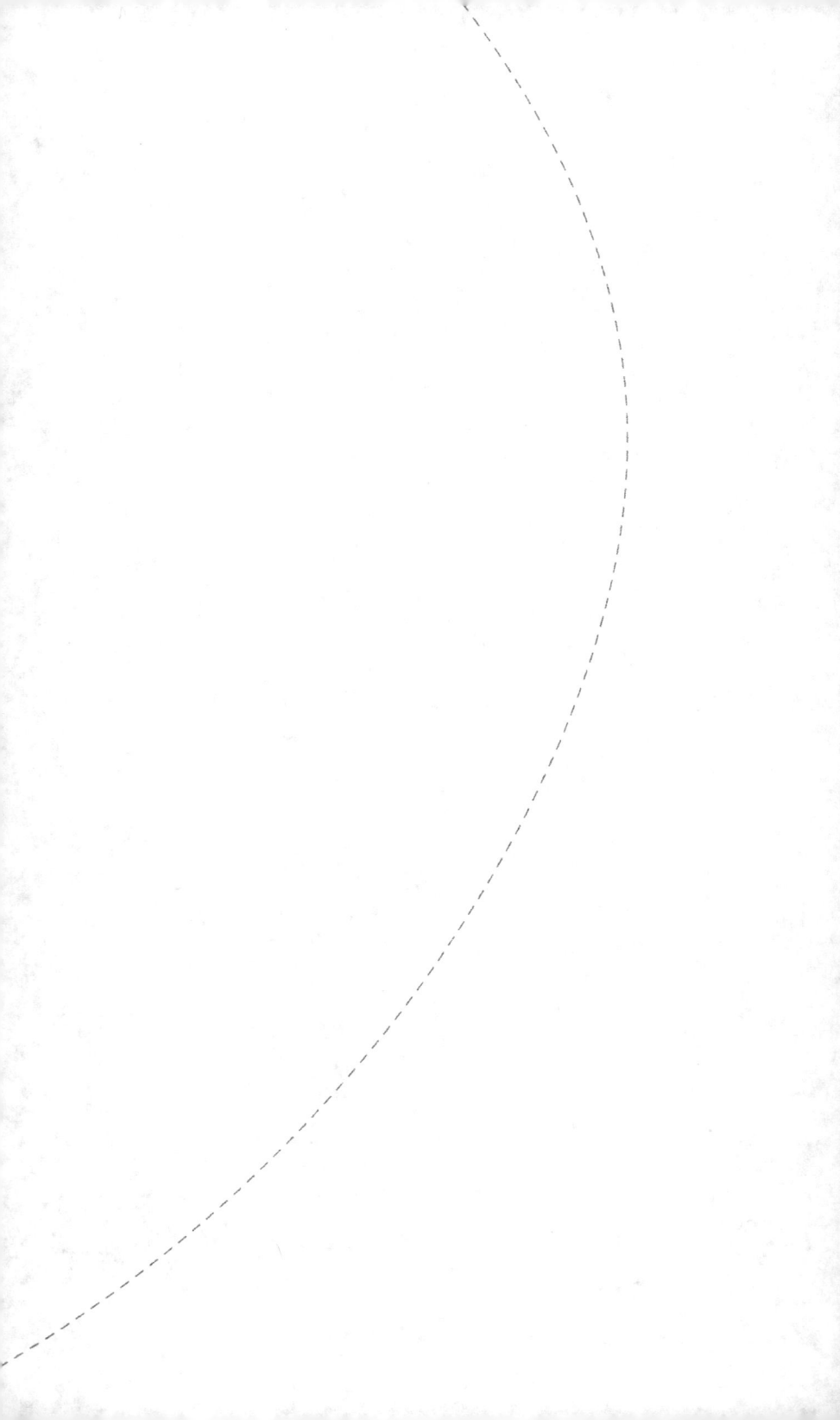

THE LONG WAY HERE

OVER TWO DECADES ago, I had a vivid dream that I still remember clearly.

It was late on a frosty winter afternoon, and I found myself in the backseat of a yellow cab in New York City, stuck in traffic. With each passing moment, I grew more frantic—my very first book signing was imminent, and I was going to be late.

When the cab finally pulled up in front of the small corner bookstore, I hurriedly paid the driver. There, in the window, I saw my book propped on a table, surrounded by people. I was dressed to the nines—wearing long Italian leather boots, a Brooks Brothers camel hair coat, and my hair styled perfectly in a French twist. As I stepped out of the cab and splashed through a small puddle, I noticed remnants of a recent snowstorm still clinging to the sidewalk.

When I awoke the next morning, I reflected on the dream. It didn't *feel* like just a dream—it felt like a glimpse of a future I was meant to create. Looking at myself in the mirror, I noticed my short hair and realized it could never be styled into a French twist. In that moment, I decided to grow my hair long in anticipation of the future I envisioned.

I've worn my hair long ever since—and that prophetic dream has finally led me here, writing this book. The path to this moment wasn't direct. It has felt lengthy, often twisted, and full of detours—some joyful, others painful. But every turn has offered lessons. Every personal and professional experience, even the difficult ones, has shaped me into the person and leader I've become.

I've been a leadership coach for six years. During that time, in leadership coaching conversations, I've shared many personal stories with my clients—hoping to spark new awareness and inspire growth. I've observed again and again that well-told stories prompt action and reflection that facts alone rarely achieve.

I've learned, too, that our personal lives and professional responsibilities are completely intertwined—like strands of DNA. In my coaching engagements, I always explain to clients that no topic is off the table. While many come into coaching expecting to focus solely on professional growth or workplace challenges, I've found that creating space for personal topics often leads to the biggest breakthroughs.

When a client is grappling with a relationship issue, such as caring for an ailing parent, supporting a child through a tough time, or navigating something personal like a divorce or illness, I don't act as a therapist or a doctor—

but I can offer a space to vent, reflect, and clear their mind. That clarity often allows them to show up more effectively at work. In truth, I've never coached a client who didn't, at some point, discuss a personal issue that was weighing heavily on them. And when I share my own personal stories in coaching—especially the moments when I've struggled to find my way through—it often gives clients the permission and courage to open up more fully.

Cognitive psychologist Jerome Bruner, once a professor at Harvard University and NYU, found that facts are up to twenty-two times more likely to be remembered when they're shared through a story. Stories give context, emotion, and meaning to information, which is a pivotal reason we retain it. I've seen this truth reflected in how often friends and clients tell me they can recall the stories I've told them months, and even years, later.

Not long ago, I began keeping a list of my most-shared stories. One day, I realized: Maybe there is a book here. Clients had told me of the stories' usefulness, after all. Naturally, more questions then arose: Who is my audience? How can I connect these stories to make them even more meaningful? What would make this collection the most helpful for the largest amount of people?

Inspiration struck when I recalled a quote from Steve Jobs in his 2005 Stanford commencement speech:

> You can't connect the dots looking forward; you
> can only connect them looking backwards. So, you

have to trust that the dots will somehow connect in your future. You have to trust in something: your gut, destiny, life, karma, whatever. Because believing that the dots will connect down the road will give you the confidence to follow your heart, even when it leads you off the well-worn path. And that will make all the difference.

Twelve years ago, while working at Merck, I was asked to introduce myself at a quarterly town hall using just one PowerPoint slide. I knew I wanted to do something memorable, so instead of a bulleted résumé, I created a "personal journey" map—complete with blue butterflies representing key moments of transformation in my life (shown in full at the end of this book's first story). That visual narrative connected my dots from childhood to the present. And my intention must've worked; many former colleagues tell me they still recall the slide with those blue butterflies to this day.

I've long considered the blue butterfly to be a symbol of transformation, change, and rebirth in my life. Many also see it as representing love, joy, and hope. I've always loved the color blue—it evokes a sense of trust and calm—so it's natural that I chose the blue butterfly for my symbol of transformation. And the butterfly's journey from a humble caterpillar to something beautiful reminds me that real change takes time and courage. Its fluttering feels spontaneous and free, much like how I try to move through life, open to change and unafraid to evolve.

Recently, while visiting a butterfly farm in Aruba, I spent hours witnessing the slow, miraculous process of transformation—watching chrysalises unfold into vibrant life. To be present in such moments was a form of mindfulness. And it reminded me of the countless times I, too, have had to shed part of one life to step into another.

In that moment, I knew my audience, knew my purpose, and knew my message. As Trina Paulus wisely wrote: "How does one become a butterfly? You must want to fly so much that you are willing to give up being a caterpillar."

One of my deepest hopes for this book is to share stories of life, love, loss, and leadership—moments that have illuminated the long route I've taken to get here. The collection is intentionally eclectic, reflecting the unpredictable and beautiful mess of real life. Some stories are deeply personal, a testament to me practicing my own vulnerability, something I've been working on and regularly encourage my clients to do as well. The stories of loss speak to my belief that even tragedy can be transformed into meaning. The leadership stories are rooted both in my own (winding in its own right) career path and in the meaningful conversations I've shared with my coaching clients. As a whole, the collection you're about to read reveals the lessons, missteps, and moments of courage that continue to shape who I am as a leader—and as a human being. I hope they will resonate with you and remind you that you're not alone and—most importantly—that growth comes in all forms.

I hope this book inspires, comforts, and encourages you to trust yourself—and your inner voice—even more. You don't have to be perfect to lead. You just have to be real, resilient, and willing to keep showing up with intention.

Thank you for letting me walk a few steps of your journey with you. Although my original concept for this book centered on emerging women leaders, the version you hold in your hands is meant for anyone who believes in leading with heart, authenticity, and courage. At the end of each chapter, you'll find the journaling exercises mentioned earlier; consider these invitations to reflect and learn from your own stories. These journaling opportunities pull you in to the community of this book and its readers. I offer them to you with hope and with gratitude, trusting that as you connect your own dots—personal and professional—you'll begin to see the shape of your path.

Even if you've taken the long way here, you're exactly where you need to be.

Let's begin.

PART I
Life Lessons That Shape Us

THE LONG AND WINDING ROAD

IN MY TWENTIES and thirties, I felt immense pressure to have a "three- to five-year plan." They seemed to be all the rage with rising successful people. So, I created my own: By the time I turned thirty, I expected to be married, have a child, own a home, and hold a certain level of authority at work.

When I hit thirty and those plans hadn't come to fruition as I had imagined, I was surprised to find myself struggling with my self-image, even though I was working hard. I often felt disappointed, anxious, and unsuccessful.

Then one day, when I was feeling particularly frustrated and stuck and had a deep urge to break out of the rut I was in, I decided to let go of that rigid, now-outdated plan. It wasn't necessarily easy, and it wasn't right away, but eventually I was able to put aside my need for control and allow life to unfold more spontaneously. By reducing that pressure, I could be thirty—and enjoy it. I found life to be more interesting and engaging. I learned to focus on optimism, worked to silence the negative voice in my head, and began to turn anxieties into opportunities. In these ways, I was able to see every challenge as a gift.

It's my belief that remembering our milestones helps us remember what we're made of. To me, a milestone isn't just something that happened; it's a moment when I grew, when I saw myself differently, or when I found a deeper sense of purpose. I believe that when we name the milestones that matter, we start to recognize not just what we've done but who we've become in the process.

For those curious about the milestones on *my* journey, here are the key highlights:

- **Early Life:** I was born and raised in Bridgeport, Connecticut—the fifth of six children in a middle-class family with strong values. My parents were second- and third-generation U.S. immigrants. My family's roots taught me that hard work is just the beginning—purpose, courage and legacy are what truly matter.

- **Early Work:** At age nine, I began working for my father at his large Italian-American supermarket, where I developed a strong work ethic and learned the importance of customer focus.

- **College and First Marriage:** I went to a private, Roman Catholic university close to home where I studied Biology and Chemistry and was the president of my class. Toward the end of college, I met and dated a handsome, fun, loving man. We married soon after my graduation and shared a deep friendship. I believe I was seeking independence from my strict, traditional upbringing at that time—my father had often said the only way a daughter could leave his house was through marriage or death. We were young, and after three years, decided to take our lives on different paths. We parted with mutual respect and remain on good terms to this day.

- **First Corporate Job:** After college, I landed my first corporate job as an analytical chemist at General Electric (GE) in their Corporate Industrial Hygiene laboratory. At first, I was elated to have a well-paying job in my field where I was learning a lot about the latest analytical techniques. However, after three years, I realized that the routine and monotony of lab work wasn't for me.

- **Following My Instincts:** I left GE for Perkin-Elmer in Norwalk, CT—a company I felt aligned with because their work involved doing good; our instruments were used to save and improve lives, protect the environment, and assist in forensic investigations. My instincts were right. I stayed there for twelve years and learned a lot about product marketing and marketing communications.

- **Personal Milestones:** I met my second husband at PerkinElmer. He worked in Business Development, and I in Marketing Communications. We dated for several years before marrying in 1993, and moved the following month to California for his job at PE. Knowing we were only going to be in California for a couple of years, I launched my own marketing communications consulting business while also planning to start a family. My husband left PE before his temporary assignment was finished, and with that, we became more fully committed to living in California.

- **Infertility and Adoption:** In 1995, we discovered my infertility—a painful and challenging period that taught me a lot about resilience and bravery. In 1996, we began the adoption process, and the following summer we adopted Emma from an orphanage in Vietnam. Motherhood changed the way I approached work—and I became much more focused on work/life integration. Emma, who was nine months old when we brought her home, is the love of my life.

- **Career in High-Tech:** After acknowledging California to be our permanent home, I applied for and accepted a position at Sun Microsystems—a company renowned for its innovative technology and fun, risk-taking culture. There, when Emma was young and pre-school age, I had the privilege of doing a thirty-hour per week job share with a dear Sun colleague, and we managed executive leadership development programs for Sun's VPs and high-potential directors. This transformational experience allowed me to meet world-class leaders and coaches, including Scott McNealy, Marshall Goldsmith, Ken Blanchard, Ram Charan, Jeff Immelt, Colin Powell, and Clayton Christensen and enlightened me about a world I didn't know existed.

- **Expanding My Skill Set:** Two years later, I returned to working full-time at Sun and made time to commit to further professional development, becoming certified in Six Sigma (achieving Black Belt mastery) and organizational change management. These skills became career-defining and vastly expanded my professional opportunities.

- **Personal Loss and Reflection:** In four short and brutal years—between December 2004 and 2008—I endured heart-wrenching losses with the passing of my mother, nephew, brother, sister, and father. Living in California while my family in Connecticut experienced so much pain was tumultuous, to say the least. I frequently traveled cross-country with Emma to support them. I was doing a lot of self-reflection about how many hours I was working, while asking myself, *What am I doing with my life? Am I focused on what's truly important to me?*

- **A Sabbatical and Renewed Purpose:** In December 2007, following the death of my brother Tony, with whom I was very close, I voluntarily left Sun Microsystems to take a one-year sabbatical. During that time, I focused on reflection, volunteering at Emma's school, exercising, and even starting a "clothes closet" to help children in need (with my fellow volunteers, we clothed over five hundred children with new or gently used outfits). This time was a good reset for my soul.

- **New Opportunities Amid a Crisis:** In 2008, during the global financial crisis, I was ready to go back to work and expanded my job search beyond the Bay Area. This took us back to the East Coast, closer to family, where I joined Merck in New Jersey.

- **Return to the East Coast and Leadership:** In 2009, I joined Merck, excited to work for one of the world's top pharmaceutical companies. Collaborating closely with the CIO and IT leadership team, I helped drive critical transformational initiatives. I ended up working in several positions at Merck, where my experience in Six Sigma and organizational change management was highly respected. It felt great to be valued, especially after so much personal loss.

- **Embracing Leadership Coaching:** In 2016 at Merck, I had the opportunity to hire an executive coach. Over time, my coach helped me clarify my personal values and leadership brand. This experience sparked my desire to help others in similar ways. As I contemplated my future—knowing that I never wanted to stop working—I decided to pursue leadership coaching. I applied to Georgetown University's Executive Certificate in Leadership Coaching program, was accepted, and earned my certificate after eight transformative months.

- **A Niche in Coaching:** At Georgetown, I learned the importance of carving out a niche. Mine came to me fairly easily: I knew I wanted to coach women in technology, drawing on my twenty years of experience in tech companies and executive roles—despite never studying technology in school. I loved the energy that women brought to the tech field and believed that by focusing on leadership presence and abilities, women in tech could aspire to higher-level positions. (I now also coach men and cherish all my clients.)

- **A Bold New Chapter:** In 2019, I voluntarily left Merck to launch my coaching practice. I still consider this a bold, gutsy decision driven by passion. I left behind a job and company I loved, even amidst personal challenges like divorce and financial commitments, to connect my purpose with my work. I named my company Prossimo, the Italian word for "next"—and have spent the last six years coaching my clients to identify their strengths and challenges in the present and embrace what's ahead for them in the future.

- **Lifelong Learning and Embracing Change:** I've learned two important things about what motivates me: that I love change and that when I'm not learning, I seek it out. Peter Senge once said, "Real learning gets to the heart of what it means to be human. Through learning, we re-create ourselves. Through learning, we become able to do something we never were able to do." Six years into my coaching practice, I feel more fulfilled than ever. And the reason is my clients.

My life-journey has taught me that progress doesn't follow a straight line. Instead, it's a series of unexpected turns and transformations. By letting go of rigid plans, embracing change, and focusing on growth, I've been able to connect the dots in ways I never imagined—and experience some pretty great side-tracks. I now celebrate every twist and turn as part of the unique path that has led me to where I am today.

I encourage you to do the same.

JOURNALING EXERCISE
Map Your Winding Road

Imagine your life as a long, winding road, filled with unexpected turns, hills, valleys, rest stops, and milestones. To see an example, find my journey map on the following pages. Rather than writing a traditional story, I'd like you to *draw* and *label* your journey using the following steps:

1. **Sketch Your Path:** On a blank page, lightly sketch a road that twists and turns. It doesn't have to be artistic or perfect—just a loose, flowing line that moves across the page. Perhaps start in one corner and weave your way to another.

2. **Mark the Milestones:** Along your winding road, add *landmarks,* where important events occurred. These could include:

   - Achievements (graduations, career milestones, personal victories)
   - Relationships (friendships, marriages, births, losses)
   - Turning points (career changes, moves, new discoveries)
   - Challenges (setbacks, grief, hard decisions)
   - Moments of growth (when you learned something about yourself or the world)

   Feel free to use small symbols, words, or little drawings at each point. Let your creativity loose. And take as long as you'd like.

3. **Label the Unexpected Turns:** Identify the moments when your path *shifted* in ways you didn't plan or expect. Did anything that awaited you around the bend surprise you? What new doors later opened because of those turns?

4. **Reflect:** After your map feels complete, answer these questions:

   - What themes or lessons do you notice along your road?
   - What events, achievements, or relationships are you most proud of?
   - How do you feel looking at your road as a whole?

5. **Title Your Map:** Give your road a title that captures the spirit of your journey so far. (Examples: *A Life Unfolding, My Story: Dot-to-Dot, Following My Inner Compass, Becoming Me*)

GENTLE REMINDER

Your journey is unfolding exactly as it's meant to—in the only way it can. You don't need to follow a straight line to build a beautiful life. Every twist, turn, and unexpected detour is shaping the remarkable person you're becoming.

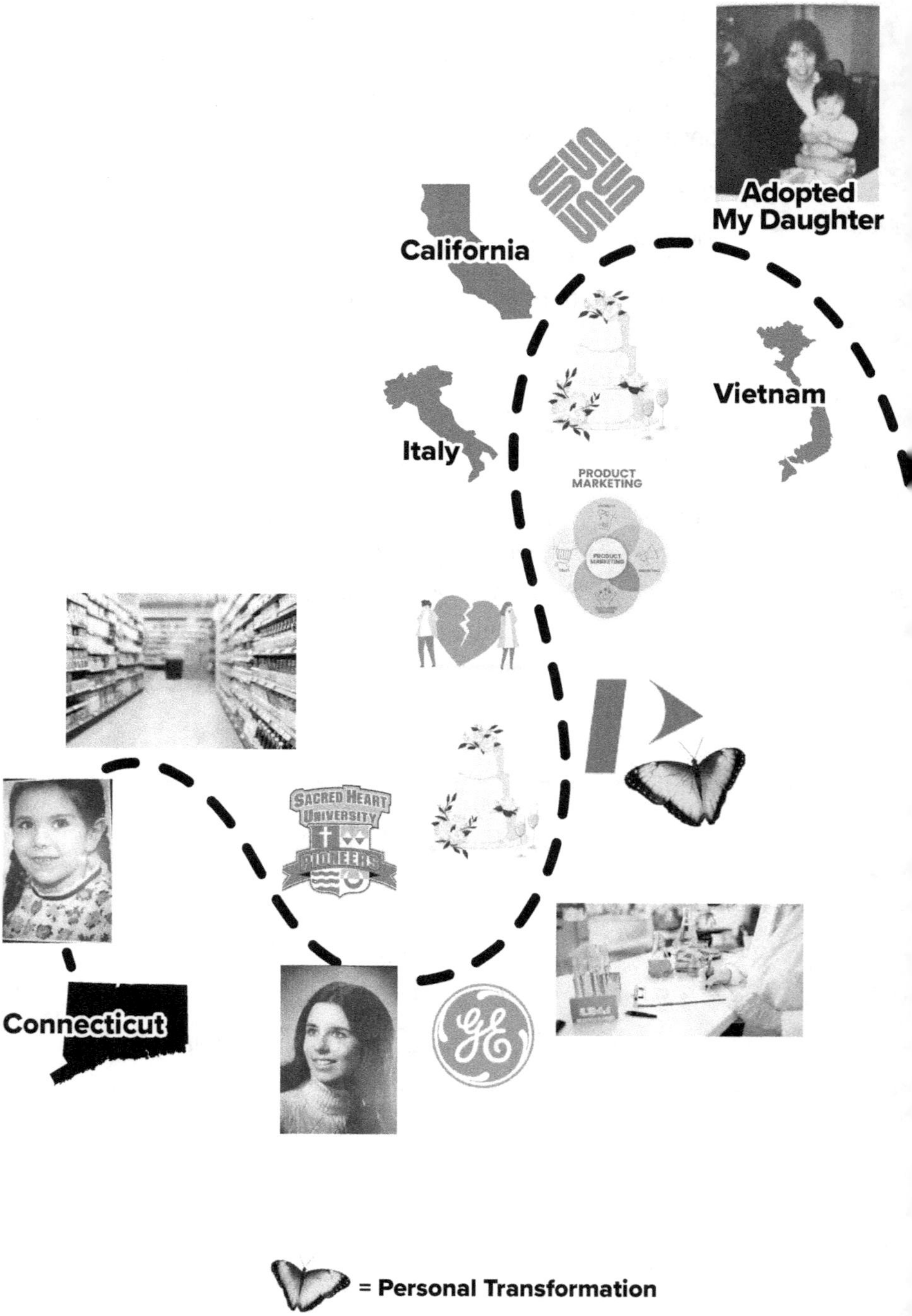

California

Adopted My Daughter

Vietnam

Italy

PRODUCT MARKETING

SACRED HEART UNIVERSITY PIONEERS

Connecticut

 = **Personal Transformation**

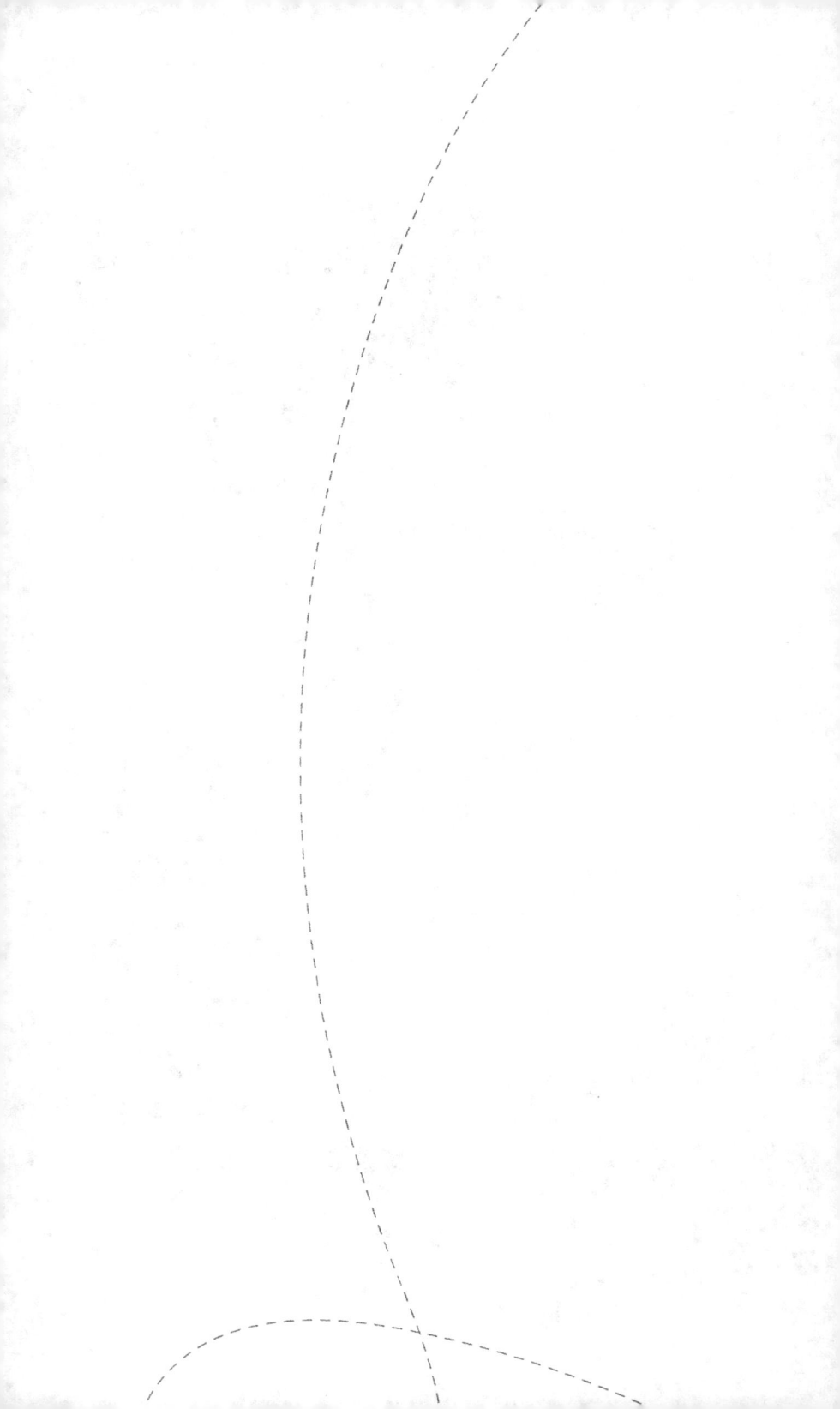

WHAT WOULD YOU CHANGE?

AS THE OLD saying goes, the only constant in life is change. It certainly has been in mine.

Let's talk numbers. I've worked for four global companies, moved twelve times and crisscrossed the U.S. twice, been married twice, and divorced twice. I've lost four siblings, two parents, four grandparents, and several nieces and nephews. I've reinvented myself many times more than all of that put together.

Time and again, I've been reminded about the importance of change. Just when you think you're all set— something shifts. Being resilient, adaptive, and optimistic— and seeing the proverbial glass half full—are traits that have helped me stay afloat. I've learned how to make lemonade out of *very* sour lemons. Most importantly, I've learned the value in keeping perspective.

But not all changes "land" easily. My move to California in 1993 shook me to the core. It wasn't just one change—it was a cascade of rushing changes. I had just gotten married, changed my last name, left the state I grew up in, said goodbye to the family I cherished, and walked away from my job and my closest friends. I landed in California only barely knowing a handful of people from old work trips. Although the honeymoon period should be the time of anyone's life, I was miserable. I had given up so much all at once, and the greatest loss of all was my identity. Who was I anymore? I felt displaced, confused, and lacking motivation—characteristics so unlike me.

Every trip back to Connecticut after living in California felt both grounding and disorienting. I was homesick for a version of myself that no longer existed. The streets were the same, but I moved through them like someone watching their life from the outside. I wanted to be there—to be close to family, to memory—but I also dreaded what it might stir in me. So much had changed. I had changed. I was no longer the woman who had left, and I wasn't yet sure who I had become.

Six months later, I found myself in a therapist's office. My therapist shared a metaphor I've never forgotten. She said, *"Families are like carnival carousels. Each horse has its place, its rhythm. When you leave, you step off the carousel. But when you return, they expect you to jump back on and ride the same horse you always did. The problem is the saddle doesn't fit you anymore."*

She helped me understand that each one of those changes—new marriage, new name, new home, new job, loss of proximity to family and friends—was its own *loss*. And loss, she reminded me, must be grieved one layer at a time. I had been trying to grieve them all at once, in a messy emotional batch that felt impossible to sift through—and I was completely overwhelmed.

That twist in the road taught me that change, even when chosen, still carries grief. And that honoring what we've lost is a necessary part of becoming who we are.

As I've grown older, I often reflect on the question: *"If you could go back and change one thing in your life, what would it be?"* Now, after everything—even the pain of that first move and the ones to come—my answer remains the same: nothing. Not because it was easy. It wasn't. But because if I went back and changed even one detail, I'd set off a domino effect of difference. I wouldn't be who I am today. I wouldn't be where I'm meant to be, which is *here, now.* I've managed to find peace and happiness, neither of which came from having a perfect, easy past or path. Today, I choose to be okay with how change shaped me.

I try to stay present, to focus on the now—but I'll admit, the fear of the unknown still sometimes creeps in. The future feels shadowy. Yet, I come back to the breath. One. Two. Three. Four.

The best thing we can do to embrace a happy future is to let go of the past. To embrace a peaceful present, we must stop worrying about what's to come. The only time we truly have is now. Let your heart fill with happiness as you notice the beauty around you. Take moments to be grateful—for your life, your winding path, and the people walking alongside you.

JOURNALING EXERCISE
Considering Change

In the Present:

1. What changes are you navigating right now—in your work, your relationships, or within yourself?

2. How are these changes affecting your energy, focus, or sense of stability?

3. Is there anything you need to acknowledge or let go of to feel more grounded, more present?

Looking Ahead:

1. When you think about the next year, what would you like to feel more of—ease, clarity, connection, purpose, or a combination of these?

2. What small shifts could help you move in those directions?

3. What support or practices might help you stay focused as things continue to change? How will you go about finding these?

GENTLE REMINDER

You don't need to have loved every part of your journey to be proud of how far you've come. Embrace change. It's not a setback—it's how you grow into who you're becoming.

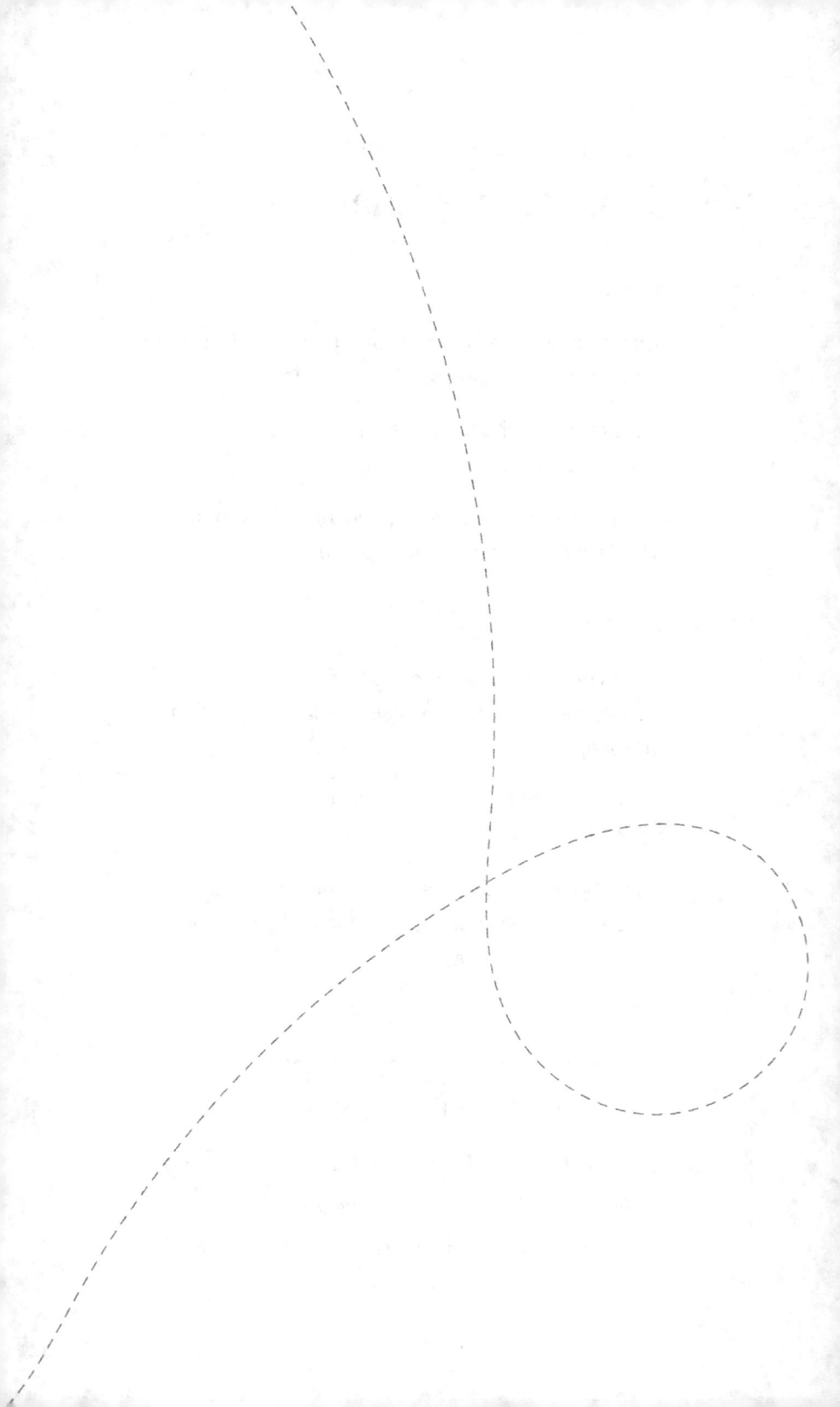

GEMMA'S MBA FROM THE AISLES OF MY FATHER'S GROCERY STORE

BEFORE I EVER stepped into a boardroom or coached a leader, I earned my business stripes in the aisles of Gemma's—my father's Italian-American grocery store. I was just nine years old when I joined the family business, and like everyone else in our household, I had no choice in the matter. My father, a self-made man who didn't finish high school, ran a store the size of a modern supermarket on the East Side of Bridgeport, Connecticut—and ran it like a general commanding a battalion.

With a booming voice and relentless drive, he built something extraordinary.

Gemma's wasn't just a grocery store—it was a neighborhood institution. In addition to the full-service store, we operated a bustling catering business and a small bakery that specialized in making a delicate pastry-like cookie called the LaWanda Twist. People came for the groceries and treats—especially the hard-to-find Italian products typically only available on Arthur Avenue in the Bronx—but they stayed for the connection. My dad knew everyone by name, and everyone knew him. And on Friday evenings, it was a hoot—most likely the only store on the planet where husbands loved to shop with their wives because my dad served the men shots of whiskey in the back room.

He had high expectations—of his staff, his customers, and, especially, his children. Without exception, everyone in my family worked at Gemma's. Weekends, holidays, summers—if school was out, you were on duty. We didn't question it. It's just what we did. Through all of those years, I picked up skills I didn't even realize I was learning. How to manage inventory. How to listen to customers. How to balance urgency with empathy. What "profit and loss" meant. How to read people. I didn't know the words "stakeholder management" back then, but I lived it every day behind the cash register.

Over the years, I held just about every role in the store. I stocked shelves, rang up customers, helped in the catering business, and even learned how to butcher meat. (That last one was not my favorite, by the way.) But working at Gemma's taught me something I now recognize as essential in leadership: there's no job too small, and no role beneath you, when you're part of a team.

My father's work ethic was legendary. He put in long hours and expected everyone around him to do the same. He didn't believe in shortcuts—only in showing up, doing the work, and doing it right. My father was proud of what he'd built and even prouder that it supported not only our family but twenty-plus employees and their families too.

Of course, like all dads, he had his quirks. One of the funniest—and most telling—was his stance on weddings. In his mind, nothing—not even his children's nuptials—should interfere with business. So, he made a rule: If you wanted him to attend your wedding, you had to get married on a holiday when the store was already closed. No exceptions. My sister once challenged this rule and planned her wedding on a regular Saturday. My father, ever the businessman, told my brother that *he* couldn't attend—someone had to stay and keep the store running, and it couldn't be the father of the bride. And so, it went. My sister got married without her brother there, and my father stayed true to his principles. Harsh? Maybe. But it was his way—and it made for some unforgettable stories throughout the years.

Looking back, I realize how much of my leadership style was shaped in that store. I learned how to treat people with respect, even when they were difficult. I learned that service isn't about smiling—it's about caring. And I learned that business *is* personal—always.

Gemma's gave me a head start most kids never get. It was my first leadership lab, my first classroom, and my first bona fide experience managing complexity. And talk about multitasking! When I later entered the world of coaching and organizational change, I brought all those lessons with me—just dressed up in different language.

People are often surprised when I say I started my career at the meat counter. But honestly? That's where I first learned how to lead.

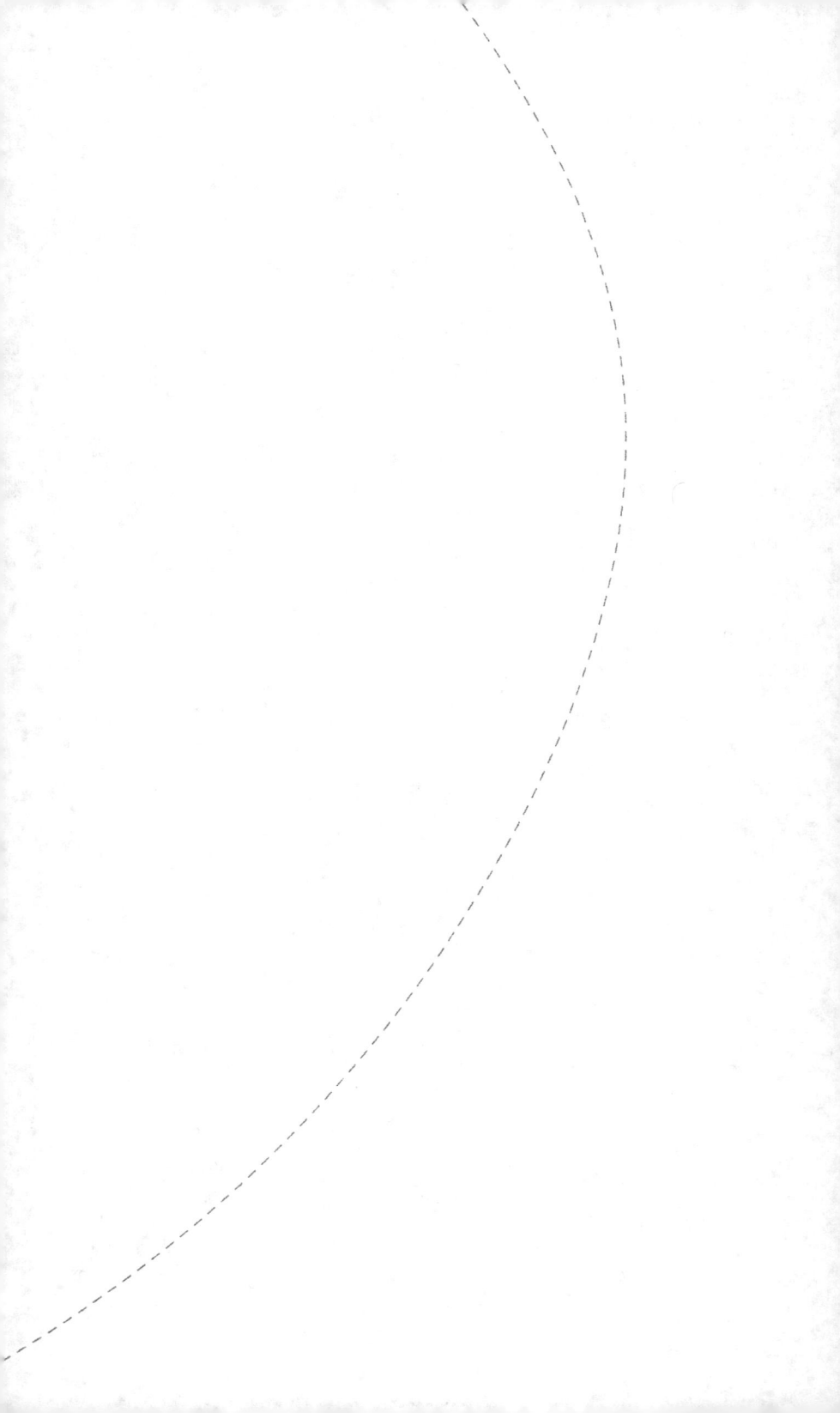

WHAT'S IMPORTANT TO YOU?

WE OFTEN TALK about our priorities, but how many of us stop to really consider which ones are *most* important? And how much time do we actually dedicate to these priorities compared to less important activities?

When I began working with an executive coach years ago, he gave me homework for one of our upcoming conversations. He asked me to write down my values. Although I assumed this would be an easy exercise, it led me to reflect in a way I had never done before. It made me acutely aware of *what* I truly value—that is, what matters most to me.

My values include love, family, independence, honesty, trustworthiness, continuous growth, respect, and humor. As I wrote, I couldn't help to reflect, which prompted me to ask myself a tough question: Am I truly living in alignment with these principles? When I paused to answer that question, I realized something surprising: How I currently lived didn't align with my values. It was as though I was being dishonest with myself. I was married at the time, but I knew deep down that my marriage was over (and had been for a long time). As I reflected further, I recognized that living a charade meant that I was deceiving myself and those around me for far too long. Eventually, I confronted my husband about our marriage, and we decided to divorce. Although the decision was mutual, I was proud of the courage it took me to face the end of a long relationship and the prospect of starting over. I knew I still had work to do. To move forward I needed to be more honest with myself to ensure the decisions I was making were tightly aligned with that mattered most to me.

By focusing on what was and is profoundly important to me, I have gained clarity about my sense of purpose and ultimately been able to align my work values with my personal values. This clarity has allowed me to notice opportunities I'd previously overlooked. For example, while working at Merck, I realized how energized I felt after coaching my colleagues and helping them focus on their personal development. I saw and encouraged "continuous growth," "honesty," and "respect," among my other core values, so my work was also *fulfilling*. These experiences eventually led me to become a full-time leadership coach and practitioner.

In my relationships, focusing on my values has helped me decide where to invest my time—and where to set boundaries. My commitment to independence has kept me from losing myself in relationships that ask for more than I can give. My dedication to respect (both ways) compels me to address any behavior that feels dismissive or demeaning, while my sense of humor helps me navigate through tough times.

Today, as a leadership coach, I encourage my clients to undertake a values exercise. I have done this with hundreds of people, and, interestingly, I have never met two with identical value sets. Having clients share their personal values and the reasons they are most important to them has been inspiring—and educational.

One of my clients, for instance, valued beauty. To this day, she's the only person I've coached with beauty in her top values. As I listened to her reasoning, I saw beauty in a new light. She didn't speak about *personal* beauty; instead, she described in amazing detail the beauty around her in the world. She shared how she loves to take walks in the park and absorb all of nature's beauty—the color of the sky, the trees, plants, flowers, birds, everything around her. As a hobby she created the most beautiful terrariums I've ever seen—filled with details that only someone who values beauty could create. I was so grateful to be her coach and learn in new ways, and I even experimented with creating a terrarium. By learning about other's values, we learn about them, which gives us the ability to understand why they behave the way they do, why they make the decisions they make, what motivates them.

I've also observed that when conflicts arise, it's usually because personal values are misaligned between two people. Remember, you can't change someone else's values, but you can choose *how* you engage with them. What I've done and encourage my clients to do is to gently name and acknowledge the misalignment. This awareness allows you to soften your response and be prepared for potential friction without being judgmental or defensive. Ideally, if you want to maintain your relationship with someone whose values are misaligned, then showing up with curiosity and understanding will help the other person feel heard and acknowledged.

Now, take a moment to think about what is important to you. Perhaps it will help to imagine you are retired and reflecting on your life and career. What advice would you give your younger self? Would you have changed anything along the way? If so, try to pinpoint what that is. Too often, we become so engrossed in our daily tasks that we fail to pay attention to our true feelings and priorities. I believe that's what makes so many of us feel as though we are living our life on cruise control.

But what if it's today, and you can still become the person you want to be? What if you could focus on what matters most to you? There's nothing saying you can't. Having clarity about what is most important is a gift you can give yourself, personally and professionally.

Clarify What's Most Important to You

For this exercise, I want you to reflect on what truly matters most in your life. Your top priorities as you seek happiness. How aligned are your daily choices with these values?

As you reflect, write about:

1. **Your Core Values:** List your top seven personal values—the principles or ideals that feel most important to you. *(Examples to choose from: love, independence, honesty, growth, adventure, creativity, respect, challenge, humor, service, beauty, achievement, family, health, etc.)*

2. **Living Your Values:** Choose one value from your list and ask yourself: *How am I currently honoring this value in my daily life? And where might I be drifting away from it?*

3. **Highlight a Moment of Courage:** Reflect on a time when living in alignment with your values required courage or a difficult decision. What did you learn from that experience?

GENTLE REMINDER

When you align your actions with what you value most, you are not just living—you are leading yourself with courage and authenticity.

FROM GUILT
TO CLARITY

ONE OF THE most beautiful gifts life gives us often arrives around the time we turn fifty. I call it the *gift of clarity*. Clarity means having a clear and well-defined understanding of something—whether it be a concept, situation, or your own thoughts and feelings. It involves understanding what you want and don't want, recognizing your needs, and making decisions that align with your values. It's the confidence to stop apologizing for who you are and to start honoring what makes you feel whole.

When I was younger, I recall trying to please everyone—never wanting to say no or hurt anyone's feelings. If an old friend called, I felt obliged to return the call immediately, even if I had nothing left to give. I cared a lot about what others thought of me and not enough about what I needed for myself. Many of my interpersonal actions were driven more by guilt than by genuine desire. After living this way most of my twenties, thirties, and even forties, I realized something: I was absolutely drained. I was over-available, under-nurtured, and disconnected from my own clarity.

But clarity, I've come to realize, isn't a lightning bolt, nor something you hope simply happens to you one day— it's a slow unfolding. It comes from living, reflecting, and being willing to tell yourself the truth.

A recent personal experience reminded me just how powerful clarity can be. I'm single now and very interested in creating a meaningful long-term relationship with a kind, fun someone. Earlier this year, I met someone I really liked. We had a strong immediate connection and shared many easy, joyful conversations. But over time, he began to pull away.

He and I had spoken previously about family and work being his top priorities, priorities that I respected. But about five months into the relationship, I found myself feeling like a lower priority, an afterthought. One morning, I sat down with my journal and asked myself, *What do I really want?* The answer poured out of me:

> My person will be someone who puts me first. That doesn't mean giving up his family or friends—it means making me a priority. Explicitly and purposefully putting me into his life. Being available for us to be together, to create memories. I want to be the first person he thinks of in the morning and the last person he thinks about at night. He

can think about everyone else in between. But I come first.

Writing those words gave me absolute clarity. In the past, I might have waited around, doubted myself, or made excuses for him. But this time, I honored what *I* needed to feel valued and safe. I sent him a note letting him know I needed to feel more prioritized if this relationship was going to work—and that if he wasn't on the same page, it might be better for us to reconsider whether to spend additional time together.

It was hard. But I had courage to choose *me*. Turns out, it was the right choice. He never contacted me after the communication. My clarity had allowed me to see his lack of interest early on, and I didn't waste time hoping this relationship might be the one.

One of my clients had a similar awakening—though hers came at work. She was a high-achieving, brilliant leader but also a true workaholic. She was not good at setting boundaries and during one of our coaching sessions, I learned she was working eighty hours a week, saying yes to every request, and drowning in deliverables. She had a young son at home, and she realized she was missing his childhood—not out of neglect but from over-responsibility in her career.

I challenged her to reclaim twenty hours a week for herself. She resisted at first, saying she felt very responsible and didn't want to let anyone at work down, but eventually rose to the challenge after subsequent coaching conversations. She began taking walks with her husband, having dinner with her family, creating white space in her calendar to save for the people who mattered. Her son was overjoyed to have his mother around more. She saw him—and herself—in a new light. And with her newfound clarity, she began saying no to tasks that didn't serve her . . . or the business. She started working more strategically and was promoted a year later.

Clarity isn't selfish. It's transformational.

And when I think about what clarity *feels* like, I often turn to the metaphor of a diamond. Every diamond is unique, formed deep within the earth under extreme heat and pressure. Most have dozens of imperfections— blemishes or inclusions that make them one of a kind. But a diamond's value is determined, in part, by its *clarity*.

Think of your clarity as the diamond in your life. Every time you act in alignment with what truly matters to you, your clarity shines brighter. And every time you say yes to something that misaligns with your values or needs, it's adding a tiny blemish to this beautiful feature. Over time, your choices either protect and enhance your brilliance or cloud it.

Clarity empowers you to choose what—and who—you bring with you on your journey and to let go of what no longer serves you. Use clarity as your compass. Let it give you permission to be who you want to be. The gift of clarity doesn't have to be a luxury of age—it's available to anyone, at any time. Clarity is achievable to you, too, but it takes a practice of courage and the readiness to ask, *What do I really want?*

JOURNALING EXERCISE
Defining My Clarity

Answer these questions about your own clarity—or your quest for it.

In the Present:

- Where in your life right now are you saying yes out of guilt, obligation, or fear of disappointing others?
- What is one situation or relationship that feels out of alignment with your values or needs?
- What would honoring your clarity look like in that area?

Looking Ahead:

- If you were to lead your life with clarity over the next ninety days, what would change?
- What boundaries would you set—or reset? Or simply polish?
- What's one decision you could make this week that reflects what really matters to you?
- Consider a long-term situation or future decision you'd like a little clarity on. Make notes about what you hope to determine in the next few years.

GENTLE REMINDER

Clarity doesn't come from figuring everything out—it comes from listening to yourself and honoring what you already know deep inside. You don't need to justify your truth. You just need to live it.

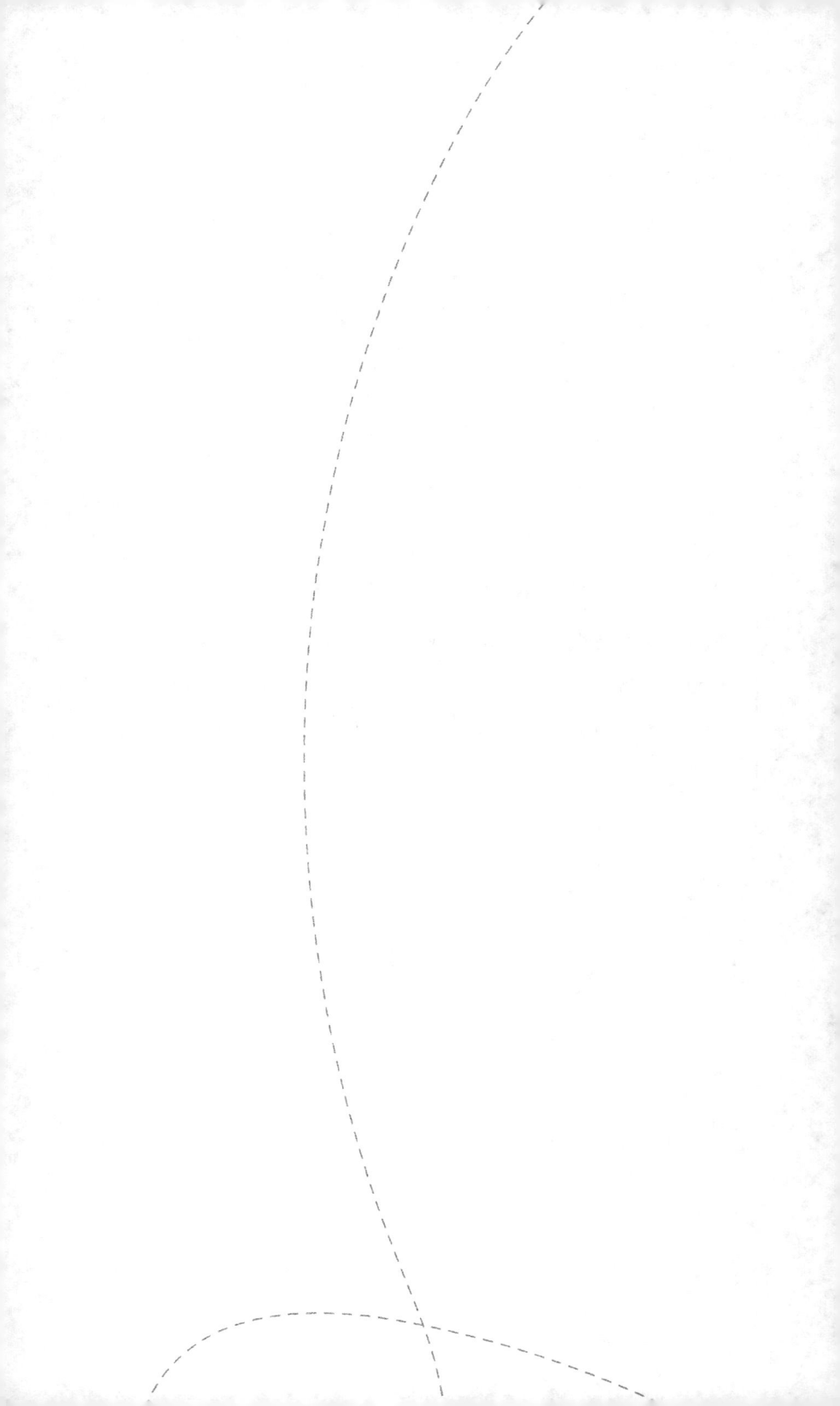

MY LIFE HAD A
FLAT TIRE

I THOUGHT I had my life together—until I saw it laid out like a pizza pie and realized one big slice was completely missing.

During an education lesson while I was attending Georgetown's Executive Leadership Coaching Program, one of the master coaches introduced me to a tool called the *Wheel of Life*.

Imagine a large circle, like a pizza pie with eight slices—each one representing a key area of life: purpose/contribution, work/career, family, romance/love, finances/wealth, friendships, spirituality, and health/fitness. By scoring how satisfied you feel in each area, you quickly see where things are thriving—and where they might need attention.

At first glance, this seemed like a simple exercise. But the moment I started filling it in, it felt like someone had handed me a mirror. What I saw staring back at me was clear: This wasn't a pie. It was a *wheel*. And mine had a serious wobble.

I scored myself high in most areas, but in the category of love/romance, I gave myself a zero. Not a one, two, or three—a big fat *zero*. From the outside, things in my life looked fine. But in an area that connected to one of my deepest *values*, I was cruising through life on a flat tire.

That day sparked a quiet but powerful shift in me. I realized I needed to act if I wanted to live the life I truly desired. I needed to make space for love. So, I did something I once swore I'd never do—I joined an online dating site. Filling out my profile and selecting photos to share with complete strangers was vulnerable and humbling. But once I posted it, I was a little relieved to see that messages and likes started coming in. (And I learned something else about myself—I was *picky*.)

A few weeks later, I went out for dinner with a friend at our local tavern. We sat at the bar and started chatting with a couple who radiated love. When I asked where they had met, they said online—and that they had recently married after just one year of dating. I felt so hopeful hearing their story.

Then I asked the woman how many men she met before finding him. Her answer? *Fifty*. Suddenly, my hopefulness turned to dread. At the pace I was going, it could take years. And then the pandemic hit, adding a whole new wrinkle to my wannabe love story. To put it simply, I had more time than ever to think about why this value was so important to me. I discovered it was not that I "wanted a man"; it was because I craved connection and companionship—someone with whom I could share the joys of life.

Now, five years later, I still have not met my person. I've let go of online dating—it no longer suits me. My new strategy is to meet someone organically. When I went to Naples, Florida, this winter, I was convinced Mr. Right was waiting there for me. After all, Naples is a mecca of older gentlemen. But here's the interesting part: While I did not meet my person in Naples, in the deepest part of my beautiful, beating heart, I *still* believe he's out there. And I'll have fun getting to know my evolving self—and all the other parts of my wheel—until we meet.

I know *me* better because of the Wheel of Life. And I want that for you, too.

The beauty of the Wheel is that it strips away complexity and helps you see your life as an entire system. It reminds you that success in one area does not mean much if another is being neglected. The Wheel reminded me that a well-lived life is not about doing everything—it's about not forgetting the parts that matter most.

JOURNALING EXERCISE

Where's My Flat or Wobbling Tire?

1. **Download or draw a blank Wheel of Life with eight slices (or create your own categories).**
   Label each section with an area that matters to you (see the first page of this story for examples).

2. **On a scale of one to ten, how satisfied are you with each area of your life?** Mark each score on the wheel and shade in the slices to match.

3. **Step back and take a look.** What do you notice? Where are you thriving? Where might your wheel be a little wobbly or flat?

4. **Choose one area that scored lower than you'd like.** What's *one small action* you could take this week to give that slice a little more attention?

5. **Finally, ask yourself: What do I *want* my wheel to look like?** Write a few sentences about what balance and fulfillment look like *to you*.

GENTLE REMINDER

Your life doesn't have to be perfectly balanced to move forward, but noticing where it's out of alignment is the first step to real change. One small action can help you re-inflate that flat tire—and set your whole life rolling again.

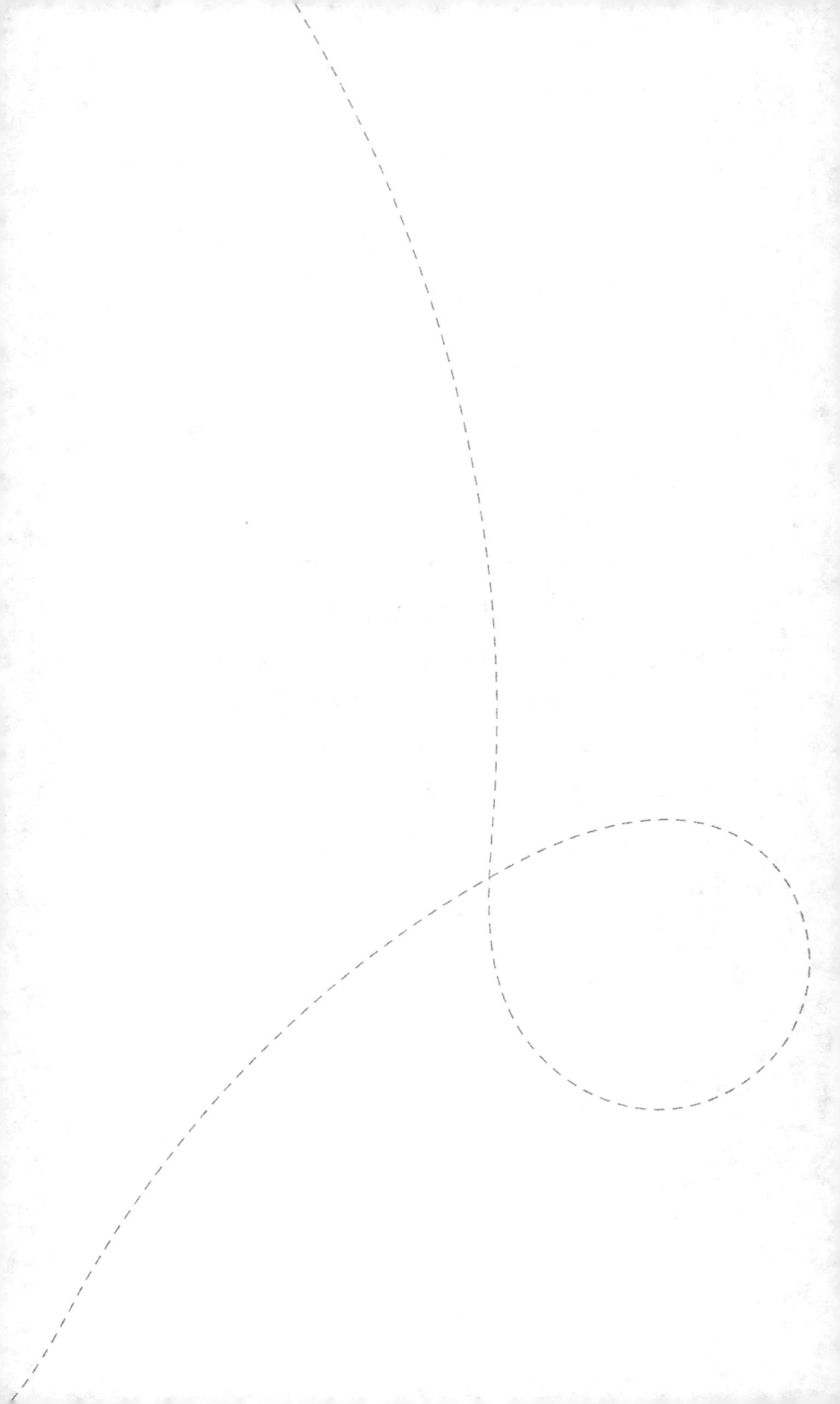

THE CEMETERY LESSON

SOME LESSONS DON'T come from books or classrooms—they come from gravestones.

In the late '80s, I learned this the hard way. Within eight months, my family lost three people we loved dearly—and they were all too young to die. A brother-in-law. A nephew. A baby niece. Each loss carried its own pain, but together they shifted something deep in me.

My brother-in-law was named John. He died suddenly of a heart attack at age forty-four, leaving my sister and her four children under the age of fifteen fatherless. My handsome, kind-hearted nephew Ray was just nineteen when we lost him to a rare form of cancer. And then came the unthinkable: the passing of Jamie, my baby niece, at the age of two. She had suffered for more than a year with a nonmalignant brain tumor, undergoing countless surgeries and procedures. We had had so much hope for her recovery. Her unfortunate death left my younger sister and brother-in-law childless and left us all heartbroken beyond words.

We were a close-knit family, shattered by grief. One funeral followed another. The sadness was so thick it felt like air we had to wade through. And while the world outside was full of headlines—Reagan's Berlin Wall speech, Black Monday, war threats, and the AIDS pandemic—my personal world had gone still.

And my professional world? At the time, I was leading marketing communications, advertising, product publicity, and sales-lead generation at PerkinElmer in Norwalk, CT. I directed a group of about thirty people. I worried I was not giving enough of myself. Outside of work, I was trying to be strong for my devastated family. I lived about twenty-five miles away from everyone and made the trip often—even after long workdays. Making time for myself to grieve didn't seem like an option. I often found myself crying alone in the car after late-night visits to support my mother, father, siblings, nieces, and nephews.

I remember lying in bed at night, praying for peace and clarity. I read *Why Bad Things Happen to Good People*, searching for meaning, asking myself what mattered most in life. I questioned everything—why I worked so many hours, what I was really chasing, and whether I was missing something more important.

And then one night, I had a vivid, almost surreal experience. I fell asleep heavy with grief and was swept into a dream where gravestones flashed before me like a shuffled deck of cards. Hundreds of them. The etchings on them were legible and crisp: *Loving mother. Devoted father and friend. Yankee fan. Gentle soul who made a difference in my life.*

When I awoke, I remembered the dream vividly. What struck me was what wasn't there. Not a single gravestone mentioned a job title. Or a company. Or how many years someone had worked. They spoke only of the relationships—the love, the laughter, the kindness, and the impact people had on others. That one dream gave me a kind of clarity I had not found anywhere else. It's stayed with me ever since, and its legacy has become a part of my core values.

While I've always had a strong work ethic and taken pride in giving my best, that night reminded me of what *really* matters. The Cemetery Lesson is always with me: Keep life in perspective. When we are gone, it's not our productivity that's remembered—it's how we made people feel. I urge you to embrace the Cemetery Lesson too.

Over the years, I have shared this story with clients who find themselves overwhelmed by the pressures of performance, titles, and expectations. We can all get easily swept up in the doing. But when I ask them to consider what they want to be remembered for—not on LinkedIn but in life—they pause. The answers are always the same: kindness, love, impact, relationships, presence, heartfelt memories. Our real work is learning to live in alignment with our values—not someday but *now*. Because in the end, it's not about how impressive our résumé is nor how hard we worked but about how deeply we've loved, how well we've shown up, and how fully we've lived.

JOURNALING EXERCISE
What Will My Inscription Be?

Imagine your life through the eyes of those who love you—your family, your friends, your community.

What will they remember most? What legacy will you leave, not in titles or achievements but in the ways you made people feel?

1. **The Heart of My Legacy:** If someone wrote a short sentence about me today—like an inscription—what would it say?

2. **What Truly Matters:** What moments, relationships, or personal qualities are most important to me now?

3. **Living with Intention:** What small change could I make starting today to live more fully aligned with the legacy I want to leave?

GENTLE REMINDER

In the end, it won't be the hours you worked or the accolades you earned that define your life's legacy. It will be the love you gave, the kindness you shared, and the moments you created that will live on forever.

PART II
Courage Through Love and Loss

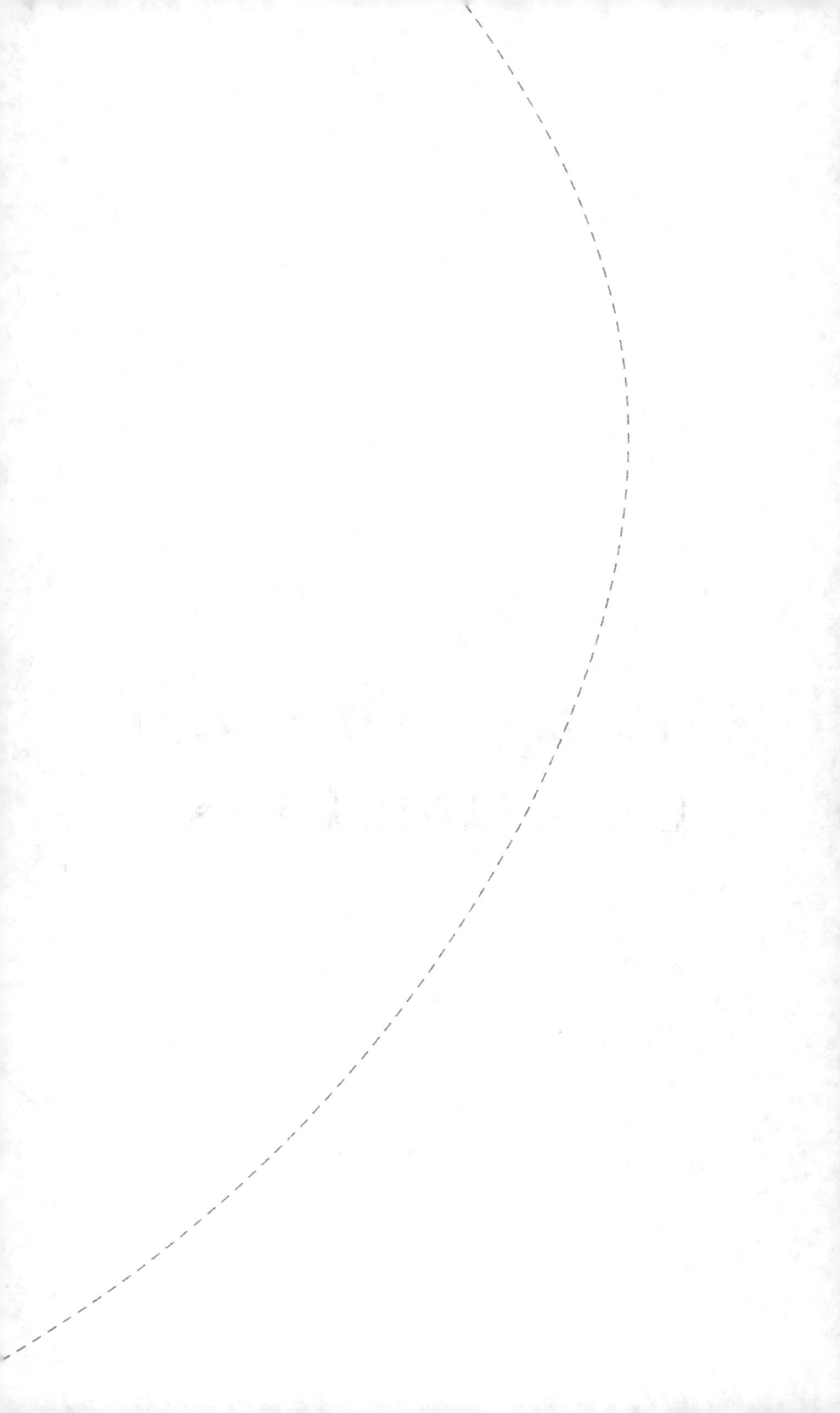

THE RESILIENT RABBIT

When the Heart Finds Its Way Home

IN ELEMENTARY SCHOOL, I remember playing a game in which the teacher asked us, "If you were an animal, what would you be?" I replied, "I would be a rabbit," because I recalled my mother once saying our family was like rabbits. At the time, I didn't fully understand what she meant. Years later, I looked it up and learned that rabbits are among the most resilient (and reproductive) animals in the kingdom. They have a thirty-day gestation period and typically produce litters of four to twelve babies, depending on their breed. Once the babies are born, the doe can mate and become pregnant again as soon as the following day.

My mother's quip made perfect sense to the older me—it was so aligned with my family. My mother was one of nine children, and my father was one of seven. My grandparents also came from large families. I was one of six

children, and each of my siblings went on to have four or
five children each, so I have twenty-two nieces and nephews
whom I deeply love. And I have twenty-eight first cousins.

With this backdrop, I always assumed that, when the
time was right, I would have a litter of children like the
rest of my family. You can imagine my shock when, in my
mid-thirties, I discovered that I was infertile. I was devastated to lose the vision of myself I'd created. I was a *rabbit*—
how could this be?

After a year of unsuccessful infertility treatments,
my doctor suggested that I stop trying—that it was doing
more harm than good to my mental health. It was one
of the saddest days of my life. I remember leaving the
doctor's office alone, doing my best to hold back the tears
that were coming. I could not get into my car fast enough
and, when I did, ended up sitting in the parking lot for
an hour, crying desperately. Yes, I had a husband who
loved me no matter what, but I felt so alone and helpless.
And inconsolable.

I hadn't realized the negative impact these infertility treatments would have on me. The process of getting pregnant
had become a job—taking medications, watching the clock,
tracking days, measuring temperatures, all while juggling
work business trips. All of my previous hopes of conceiv-
ing a child within a loving relationship had been reduced to
a calculated, mechanical process that was neither loving nor
logical. The clinical approach had stripped away the intimacy

and joy I once felt in my marriage, leaving me isolated and disconnected from both my body and my husband.

Yet, I've always been resilient, and time has a way of healing. I shifted my focus to other things—work, gardening, friends, and cooking. One evening, my husband suddenly asked if we should consider adoption. I'll be honest: I had never given it much thought because, after all, I was a rabbit. Still, I answered him with an enthusiastic yes, and our new mission began. We were going to adopt a baby.

The next day, I started researching. We decided to adopt internationally from Vietnam. Everything we read about Vietnam's culture and how they loved and cared for abandoned babies was aligned with our family values. I called an international adoption agency in the Bay Area, and the following Saturday we attended an introductory meeting to learn more about the adoption process and next steps. The next six months were a whirlwind of paperwork and appointments. (It amazes me what adoptive parents have to go through to become qualified to parent, while fertile couples simply reproduce to have a baby.)

The process, at times, felt arduous. We attended three mandatory classes to learn what it means to be an adoptive parent of an international child; wrote a personal letter explaining what adoption meant to us and highlighting the kind of parents we would be; gathered reference letters from four friends who had known us for at least a year; underwent medical exams to prove our health; completed a home study;

and participated in background checks and fingerprinting. During this time, I remember watching the news and hearing about a mother who threw her baby from a New York City skyscraper. I began to wonder why all parents shouldn't have to go through the same rigorous process as adoptive parents. I saw everything from the other side and realized that simply being fertile isn't a qualification for parenthood.

Six months later, while on a business trip in Paris, I received a call from the adoption agency. They told me they had a four-month-old baby girl for us. We immediately said yes—we just knew she was meant to be ours! We decided to name her Emma after my husband's dear grandmother, who had lived with him while he was growing up in Italy. The next five months became a flurry of preparations for our trip to Vietnam, while we awaited travel and adoption paperwork. The anticipation of this period felt almost like a pregnancy, as we readied everything to bring our baby home. We traveled to Vietnam at the end of July and returned home in mid-August.

After adopting Emma, I truly realized how fortunate I was. This profound experience reshaped my perspective on parenthood, teaching me that love and family are not defined by biology but by the bonds we create. The journey tested my resilience and deepened my understanding of what it truly means to be a mother. As strange as it may sound, I believe adoption is part of my life's journey; I am grateful that I never had a biological child. Had I, I might have simply checked the "I have a kid" box and never considered adoption, with all of its blessings and rich layers of love. Instead, I can say with certainty that Emma was meant to be mine and I, hers. She is the light of my life—beautiful inside and out, a soul who is loving, compassionate, generous, and kind to all.

Not long after adopting Emma, a friend of mine gave me a poem by Fleur Conkling Heyliger that I have always cherished:

Not flesh of my flesh,
nor bone of my bone,
but still miraculously my own.
Never forget for a single minute,
you didn't grow under my heart, but in it.

Because of experiencing infertility, going through the adoption process, and being a mother to Emma, I've discovered new levels of *resilience*.

I have become even stronger, more determined, and a fiercer advocate for women. The winding road that led me to her was full of twists and turns I never expected. What felt like heartbreak(s) at the time turned out to be the very path I was meant to walk. Sometimes we can't see the end of the bumpy road we're on, but when we get there, we realize it brought us somewhere more beautiful than we ever could have planned.

JOURNALING EXERCISE

How Resilient Am I?

Resilience reveals itself not through easy moments but through the hardest challenges—the ones we never planned for. Reflect on a time in your life when you faced a deep disappointment, unexpected change, or loss—and found a way to move forward with hope.

For this exercise, write about:

1. **A Challenge I Faced:** Briefly describe a time when life didn't unfold the way you expected or planned.

2. **How I Found Strength:** What helped you get through it—inner qualities, people, new opportunities, faith, time?

3. **What I Gained:** Looking back, what gifts, lessons, or new perspectives came from this experience?

4. **Resilience Today:** How has that experience shaped the person you are today? In what ways are you stronger, wiser, or more compassionate because of it?

5. **Resilience Tomorrow:** What did you learn from the experience, and how will it reshape your perspective for tomorrow?

6. **A Message to Myself:** Write a brief note to yourself celebrating your resilience and courage. (Example: I am proud of the way I stayed open to love, even when life felt uncertain.)

7. Repeat the above steps for other previous challenges, as you wish.

GENTLE REMINDER

On the days that feel tender, remember that your heart stretches to hold joy and sorrow. You are growing in ways you cannot always see. Trust your inner strength. Trust your journey. You are exactly where you need to be.

TONY'S GIFTS AND THE POWER OF HOPE

MY BROTHER TONY was an inspirational person who profoundly impacted the decisions I've made in my life. When I was living in the Bay Area in California, he was on the East Coast, courageously battling pancreatic cancer—a diagnosis no one ever wants to hear, much less the family of those fighting it.

Tony was being treated at Memorial Sloan Kettering in New York City. Every Sunday, my sister-in-law would drive him to an apartment he rented on the Upper East Side so he could be close to the hospital during treatment. On weekends, he'd return to Connecticut to be with his family. He did everything he could to fight the illness—from surgery and chemotherapy to deepening his spiritual faith. For over a year, Tony battled fiercely, and there were moments when it seemed he might be one of the lucky survivors.

We spoke often during that time. I was working at Sun Microsystems in a highly visible and demanding role as Chief of Staff to the Executive Vice President of Software. I had a long, ninety-minute commute each way along Route 101, which gave me a lot of driving time to talk with Tony. I spent most of my days praying for his recovery.

A few times on my drive, I saw something both unexpected and beautiful: rainbows arcing over the valleys around me. California rarely gets rain outside of winter, so these were an odd spring- and summertime sight, especially without any rain. Those rainbows became symbols of hope for me—quiet reminders that maybe, just maybe, Tony would be okay.

Tony had always been entrepreneurial and driven—a workaholic, like many in our family. But during his battle with cancer, he became more reflective, and I had the gift of hearing his evolving wisdom. One of the most profound quotes he shared with me was about **health, time, and money**:

> Put love aside, and what's left is health, time, and money.
>
> When I had health and time, I had no money.
>
> When I had health and money, I had no time.
>
> And now, while I have time and money, I do not have my health.

The words struck me like a lightning bolt. They were simple but so deeply true. I've carried them with me ever since.

Then came the dreaded day when his doctors told him there was nothing more they could do for him. They suspected he had a few months to live—but in actuality, he passed away a few days later. I interpreted Tony's death as a lesson about **hope**: When we have hope, we have something to live for. When hope disappears, as Tony's did when he received his grim prognosis, we begin to fade.

Hope fuels courage within us in place of fear. It makes room for peace in the midst of pain, teaches us patience when we feel like giving up, and gives confidence in the face of uncertainty. Watching how hope had sustained Tony changed me forever.

After he passed in May 2007, I entered a hard season. I was still working long hours and facing that same grueling commute, all while raising a child and carrying the heavy weight of grief. I can't tell you how many times I heard Tony's voice in my head, reminding me of what really matters. By the end of the year, I made a bold decision: I left Sun Microsystems. With my husband's support, I took a self-funded sabbatical that could last for six to nine months.

It was one of the best decisions of my life.

I gave up my income—but I gained the priceless gifts of time and health. I spent more quality time with my daughter, who was in fifth grade at the time. I took my natural energy and volunteered at her school and started a children's clothing closet for the St. Vincent de Paul Society in our community. Through donations and volunteers, we helped provide over five hundred children with clothing twice a year and distributed more than one hundred new winter coats.

I also created space for joy. After school drop-offs, I carved out time to walk four to six miles, three times a week, with a dear friend. In the midst of grief, the year 2008 became a time of purpose, healing, and reconnection—with my values, my family, and my community.

Ultimately, I did go back to work the next year—even took a job on the East Coast because the role thrilled me and would put me closer to family. The company, Merck, became like a second home; eventually, I was even promoted to Executive Director. Today, nearly twenty years after Tony's death, I continue to live by his wisdom, and it's enhanced my life in so many ways, most important of which is gratitude.

I honor the balance of health, time, and money. I see all three as gifts, not guarantees. And above all, I never forget what Tony taught me in his final days: when we have hope, we have everything.

As you move forward in your career and your life outside of work, I encourage you to prioritize hope. I think hope, by the way, is the main reason I love coaching so much. At its core, coaching is about cultivating hope— helping someone imagine a future that feels just out of reach, or maybe one they never thought possible. It's one of the greatest privileges of my work, and in many ways, it's my way of continuing Tony's legacy.

JOURNALING EXERCISE
Embracing Tony's Gifts

1. **Reflecting on Health, Time, and Money:**
   When in your life have you had two of the three but
   were missing the third? How did that shape your
   choices or priorities?

2. **The Role of Hope:** Think about a time when
   hope carried you through something difficult.
   How did having hope help you? (Be specific with
   your answers.)

3. **Priorities Today:** What truly matters most to you
   right now? How are you intentionally caring for your
   health, your time, your financial well-being—and your
   spirit of hope?

4. **For Your Future Self:** What is one small change or
   commitment you can make today to honor these gifts
   more fully for your future?

GENTLE REMINDER

*Hope is not about certainty—it's about possibility. It helps
you keep moving, even when the path isn't clear. Sometimes,
just believing things can get better is the first step toward
making them so.*

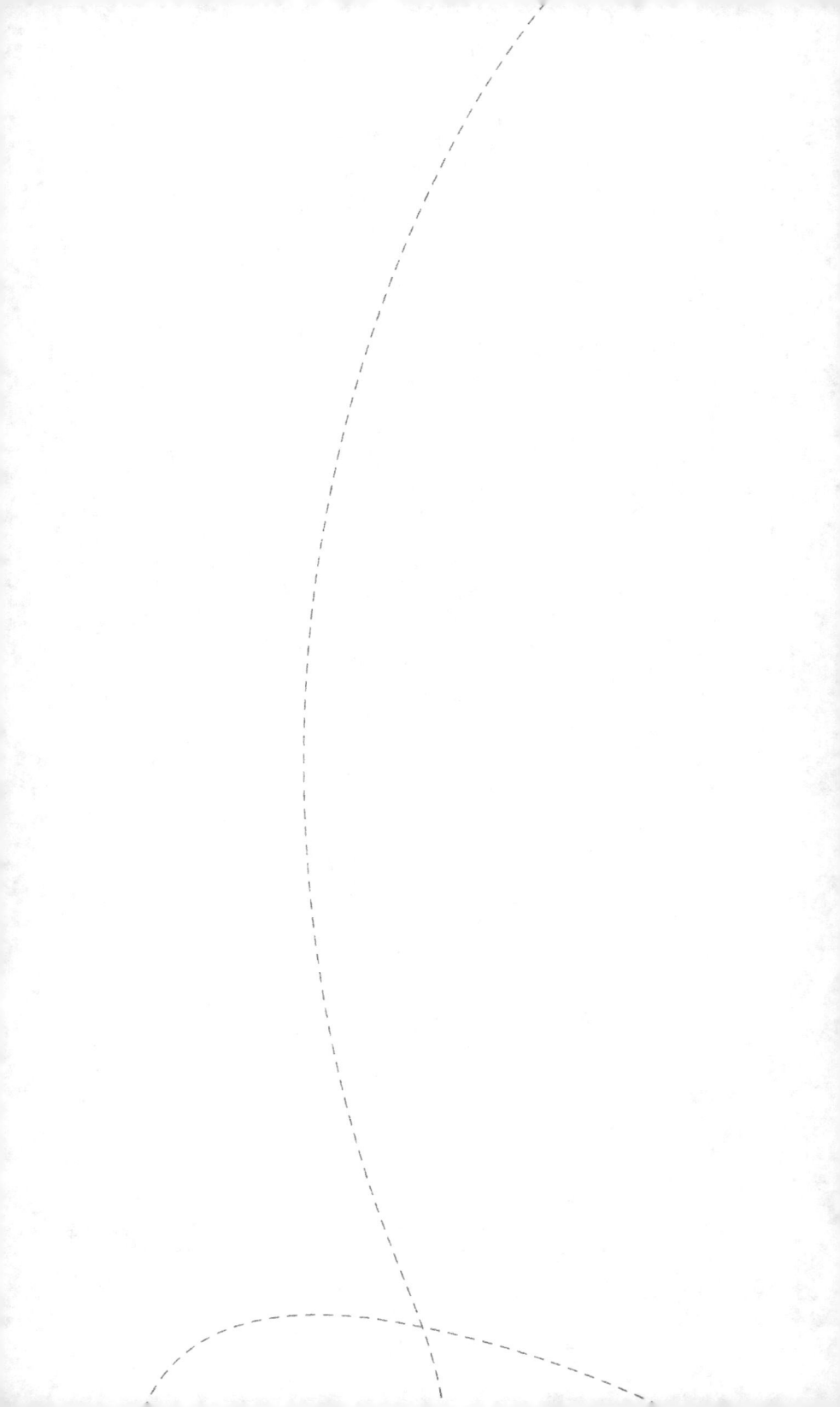

NEVER SAY NEVER

Opening the Door to Possibility

ONE THING I'VE realized about myself is that my English is very idiomatic. I've become even more aware of this while coaching clients for whom English is a second language. I catch myself using phrases such as:

Sounds like you need to *go back to the drawing board.*

Are you *fighting an uphill battle?*

Your colleague sounds like she's *cool as a cucumber.*

Birds of a feather flock together.

Take the phrase *never say never,* for instance. It means you shouldn't rule anything out completely, because life can change and so can you. At its core, *never say never* is about staying open to possibility.

Lately, I've been reflecting on that phrase. Many of the things I once insisted I would *never* do, I eventually did.

Years ago, when I was working at PerkinElmer, the East Coast–based company acquired a software start-up called Nelson Analytical in Cupertino, California. At the time, I led the company's marketing communications function and needed to travel west on a monthly basis for the integration. One day, the founder of Nelson suggested I move to California. I replied—emphatically—"I will NEVER move to California." I could never envision myself moving three thousand miles away from my family and friends for any reason and especially not my career.

Fast forward four years: I moved to California—just three miles from Nelson's headquarters. What changed? I fell in love. I met my future husband while working at PerkinElmer, and when he was asked to relocate to the Bay Area in 1993, I followed. After we settled in, we had dinner with the Nelson founder and his wife. He laughed and reminded me of my "never." Life, it turns out, has a sense of humor—and a plan of its own.

Since then, I've noticed how many of my "nevers" softened into "maybes" and eventually became "yeses." I once said I'd *never* do any of the following things: start my own business, get a divorce, online date, deliver a keynote to a huge roomful of people, run a 5K, travel solo, live in Florida—or get a tattoo. I've done all of those things. Some brought joy, some discomfort (the tattoo, for instance!), but all brought growth. And every one of them expanded me.

(The tattoo, in all seriousness, was extra special—it reaffirmed the close, evolving bond I share with my daughter, Emma. Last year, we got matching mother-daughter blue butterfly tattoos for my birthday, a meaningful reminder of how much we've both grown and how deeply we're connected, no matter where life takes us.)

Now, I can't help but ask myself: *What would it look like to take the word "never" out of my vocabulary?* What doors might open if I stayed curious?

One recent experiment came from that shift in mindset. Because my coaching work is virtual, I decided to rent a condo in Florida for the winter—to try out life as a snowbird. It wasn't a vacation; it was an intentional test of a new lifestyle. I moved to a new climate for 2.5 months where I didn't know a soul. I found joy in the sunshine, made new friends, and proved to myself, once again, that "never" has the potential to end a story before it even begins.

I often share this story with clients who feel stuck in rigid thinking or are holding tightly to a fixed path. One client comes to mind. Jennifer was feeling very stuck in her old job. She was suffering from severe burnout. As we explored a possible shift in her role and the idea of her taking some well-deserved time off, she shared a string of limiting beliefs:

"I could never work in that part of the organization."

"I'd never be good at that kind of job."

"I never take more than a week off at a time."

But as we unpacked those statements, something shifted. She realized those "nevers" were based on outdated assumptions—not truth. She wasn't resisting the opportunities; she was resisting the permission to imagine herself doing something different. As it turns out, once she gave herself that permission, new possibilities began to open—both professionally and personally.

Now, when I hear a client say, "I could never . . . " I gently ask: **"What if that's not true?"** That simple question changes everything. It moves the conversation from fear to curiosity—and from limitation to growth.

JOURNALING EXERCISE
Turning Never Into Possibility

Right Now:

- Where in your life or work do you find yourself saying, "I could never . . . "?
- What's the real story behind that belief? Is it fear, habit, or someone else's expectations?

Looking Ahead:

- What's something you've quietly dreamed of doing but dismissed as unrealistic or out of reach?
- What would it look like to explore it gently, without pressure or commitment?
- What is one small step you could take this month to test its possibility?

GENTLE REMINDER

"Never" is rarely the end of the story. More often, it's just fear in disguise. Stay curious. Give yourself permission to explore what might be possible—and let the rest unfold from there.

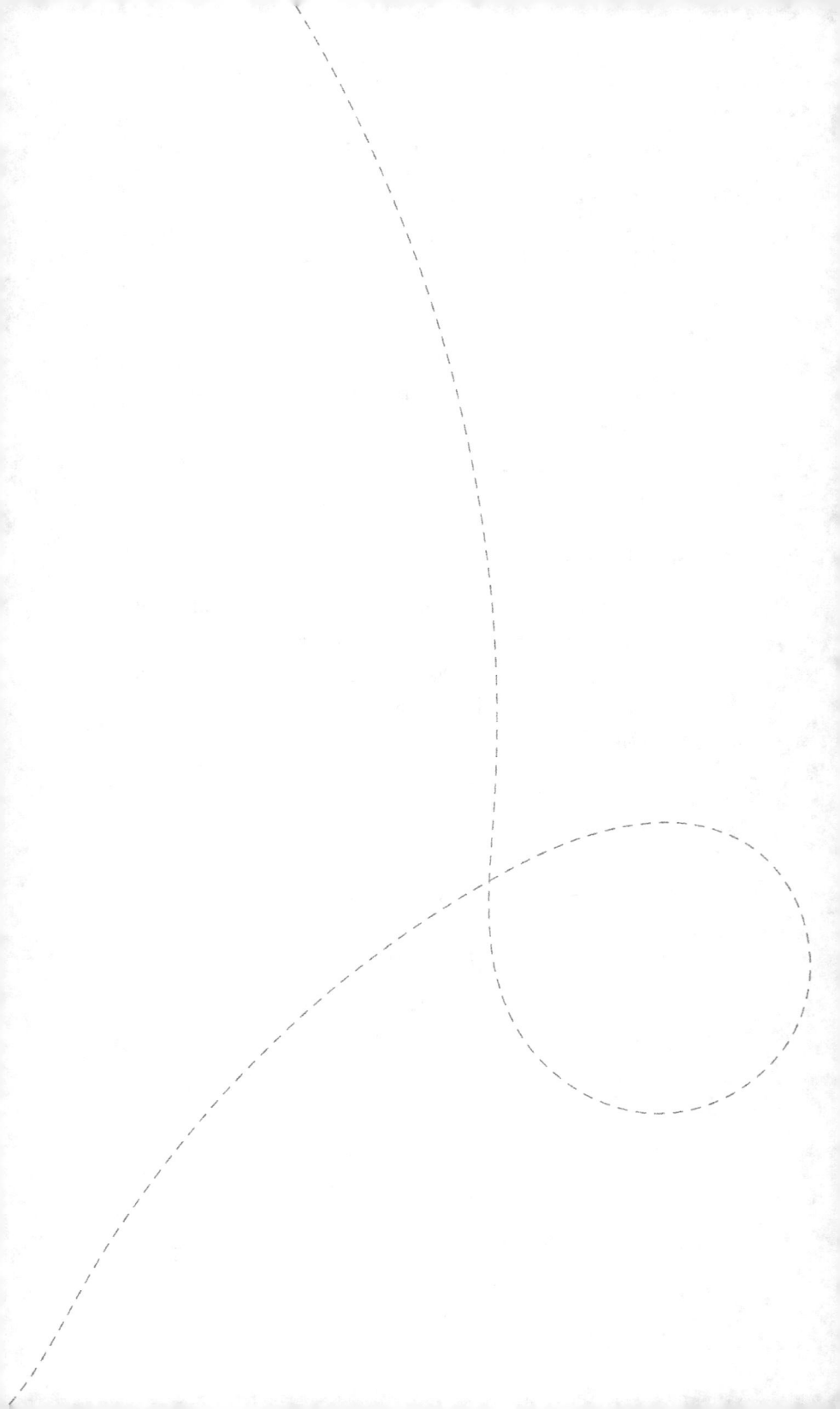

LET YOUR ENERGY BE YOUR GUIDE

ONE EXERCISE I'VE done many times throughout my life is simple—but powerful. I track what gives me energy versus what drains it. It's a reflection practice that helps me notice not just what I *do* but how it *feels*. Over the years, it's helped me reconnect with both my purpose and my personal happiness. The key is to pause—either in the moment or at the end of the day—and pay attention.

Years ago, when I was working at Merck, I had a job I loved and an amazing team. At the time, I was also working with a coach who introduced me to the idea of energy tracking. He asked me to begin keeping a journal of specific activities that left me feeling energized versus depleted. Turns out, the more detailed I was, the more useful it became.

I noticed that during one-on-one meetings—especially when I was coaching my team members on leadership, change management, or strategy execution—I felt completely alive. The hours flew by. I left the office buzzing, fulfilled, and proud of the impact I had made.

But there were other days. Days when I had to facilitate half-day governance meetings about project funding. Even the night before, I'd feel the dread creeping in—the classic "Sunday Scaries." I'd sit through those sessions feeling drained and leave completely exhausted, like my energy had been siphoned out of me.

I've felt that same depletion in personal relationships too—times when I dreaded going home, walked on eggshells, or shrank myself to avoid conflict. Those experiences were also telling me something important.

To do this exercise, the key is to dig beneath the surface. What exactly is causing you to feel depleted? Is there a conversation you could have? A request you could make? Are your values misaligned with what's being asked of you—or who you're surrounded by?

Before you can begin, you must pause, allow time in your days to reflect on your energy. Journaling can help. So can coaching or therapy, especially when the heaviness becomes hard to carry alone.

Energy awareness is also a powerful lens for career reflection. After two years of paying attention to what energized me at Merck, I began asking myself a question I had never before seriously considered: *What if I could do this—coaching—for a living?*

That question led me to apply for the Georgetown University Executive Certificate in Leadership Coaching program. Attending that program changed my life. It confirmed that coaching wasn't just something I enjoyed— it was something I was meant to do. Six years after starting my coaching business, Prossimo, I can say with full honesty: My coaching work *never* feels like work. It feels like purpose. When your work aligns with your energy, you don't burn out—you light up.

I've offered the following energy-tracking practice to many of my clients, especially those navigating career transitions or seeking more meaningful work. It's a grounding tool that helps them make decisions not just based on titles or salary but on what truly brings them alive. Again and again, they've told me how helpful it is—not only in choosing their next role but in choosing a more aligned life.

JOURNALING EXERCISE
Following Your Energy

1. **Positive-Energy Moments:** Think about a recent day or week. What activities, conversations, or experiences have given you energy—made you feel alive, purposeful, or joyful?

2. **Draining-Energy Moments:** What has left you feeling depleted, tense, or zapped?

3. **Noticing Patterns:** Are there themes in what lifts you up versus what weighs you down? What are they, and how can you find more of them?

4. **Making Small Shifts:** What is one small shift you can make—setting a boundary, making a request, saying yes to something new—to bring more positive energy into your life?

GENTLE REMINDER

Your energy knows before your mind catches up. Trust the feelings that lift you. Honor the ones that weigh you down. Let your next step be guided by what makes you feel most alive.

PART III

Owning Your Leadership Journey

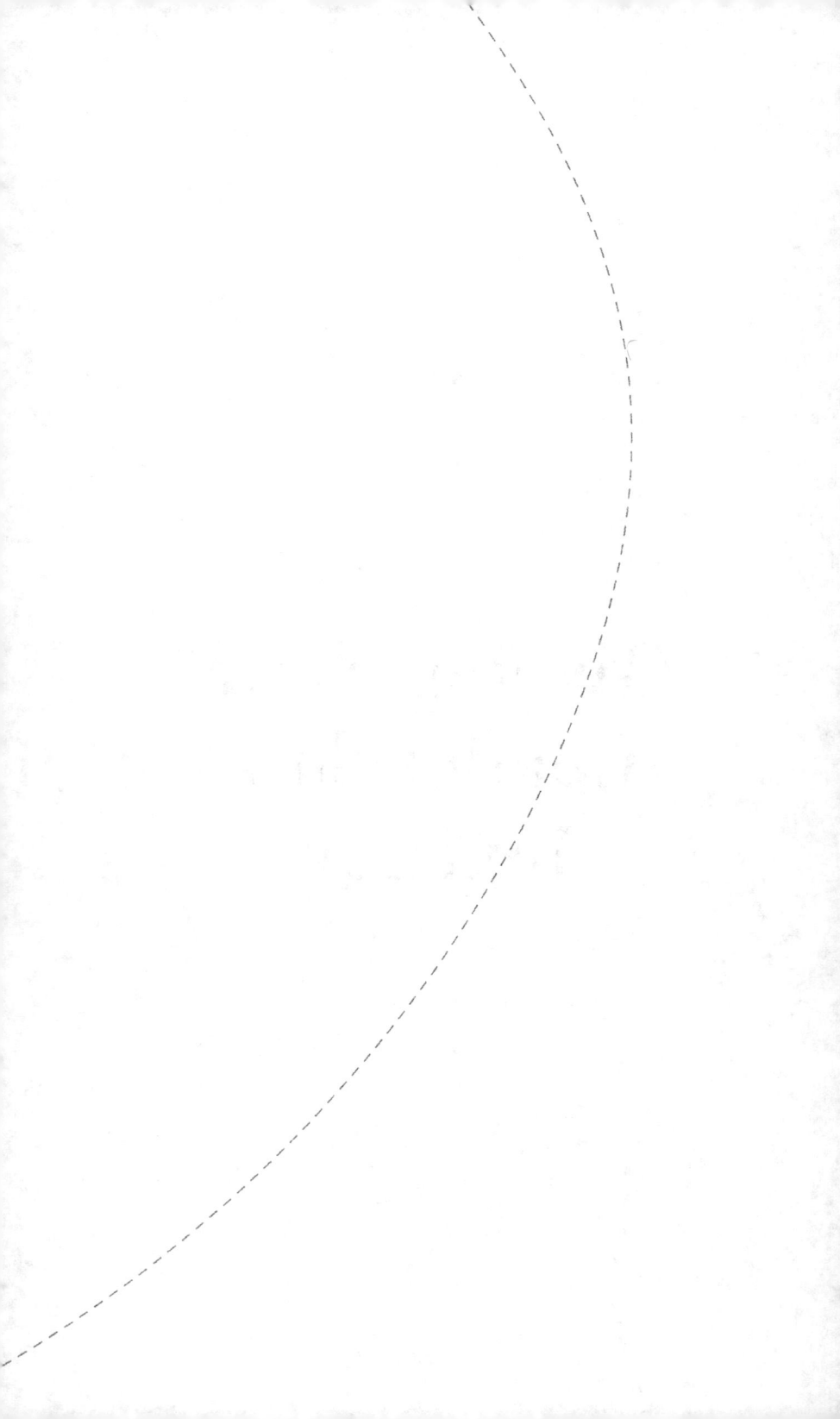

MY THREE-VALUE CAREER COMPASS

ONE TRUTH I'VE learned over the years: The architect of your own career is *you*. Not your boss. Not your company. Not the economy. You.

You get to decide who you want to be, what kind of work fuels you, and when it's time to move on. That doesn't mean it's easy—but it does mean the power is yours.

I've been fortunate to work at four major corporations over my career—and I have to be honest that I take quiet pride in the fact that I was never laid off or fired. But that also means I had to make some tough calls myself. I chose to leave each of those companies, and twice I walked away *without another job lined up.* Looking back, I recognize how bold (some may say risky) that was—especially with a mortgage and a car payment to cover among other life expenses that come with raising a child. But each time, something inside me said: *It's time.* And I trusted that voice.

That confidence didn't appear overnight. It was shaped by two pieces of advice I've worn like armor. The first came from one of my early managers: *"You are responsible for your career."* The second came from my mother: *"You are responsible for your happiness."*

Those two truths became my north stars. That manager reminded me that no one was going to tap me on the shoulder and hand me my dream job—I had to steer toward it. And my mother's words taught me that happiness is an inside job. You can't outsource it—not to a partner, not to a boss, not even to the perfect title.

Eventually, through trial, error, and some career pivots, I developed what I now call my **Three-Value Career Compass**—a kind of litmus test I use to evaluate when it's time to stay or go.

> **Rule 1:** I must be working on something the company values—and that's aligned with its strategy and priorities.

> **Rule 2:** I must have the opportunity to contribute my unique value while continually learning and growing. This is about my ability to create value for the company.

> **Rule 3:** I must feel valued—and be rewarded fairly for my contributions (compensation, benefits, recognition, respect).

When all three are present, I thrive. When even one is missing for too long, I know it's time to pay attention. This simple framework became my internal compass. It helped me navigate uncertainty, evaluate new opportunities, and make bold moves with clarity. Every time I resigned from a role, leadership asked me to reconsider. But I always left with integrity—and clarity. I'd explain, "This isn't about something the company did wrong. It's about what's next for me."

What gave me the courage to leave—especially without a safety net—was this: I had done the work. Thanks to the Three-Value Career Compass, I knew what I needed in order to feel fulfilled and energized in my career. And when that alignment started to slip, I didn't wait for things to get worse. I listened to my gut and made the leap.

I've shared this same three-value framework with many of my coaching clients—especially those feeling stuck, undervalued, or unsure of what's next. It gives them something clear to reflect on, a way to pause the noise and ask: *Where am I aligned? Where am I drifting? What do I need to feel whole again at work?*

Over and over, clients tell me how *grounding* and *clarifying* this tool is—especially when facing a career transition. It helps them make decisions not from fear but from self-worth and intention. It reconnects them to what really matters. So, whenever you feel uncertain, ask yourself:

1. Am I working on something that matters—to me and the company?
2. Am I learning, growing, and contributing my best value?
3. Do I feel valued and fairly rewarded?

If you answer "no" to any of these, it might be time to pause, reflect, and explore what's next.

JOURNALING EXERCISE

Your Three-Value Career Compass

1. **Your Three Non-Negotiables:** What are the three core values or conditions *you* must have in your career to feel energized, fulfilled, and proud? *(Examples: growth, creativity, autonomy, impact, recognition, flexibility, psychological safety)*

2. **Check-In:** How aligned is your current role with these values? Where are you thriving—and where might you be drifting?

3. **Inner-Voice Reflection:** When have you trusted your inner voice in your career? What happened when you acted on it? When you didn't listen?

4. **Looking Ahead:** What bold or courageous step might your future-self thank you for?

GENTLE REMINDER

No one else can build the future you desire. Own your worth. Honor your values. Lead your career with clarity, courage, and heart.

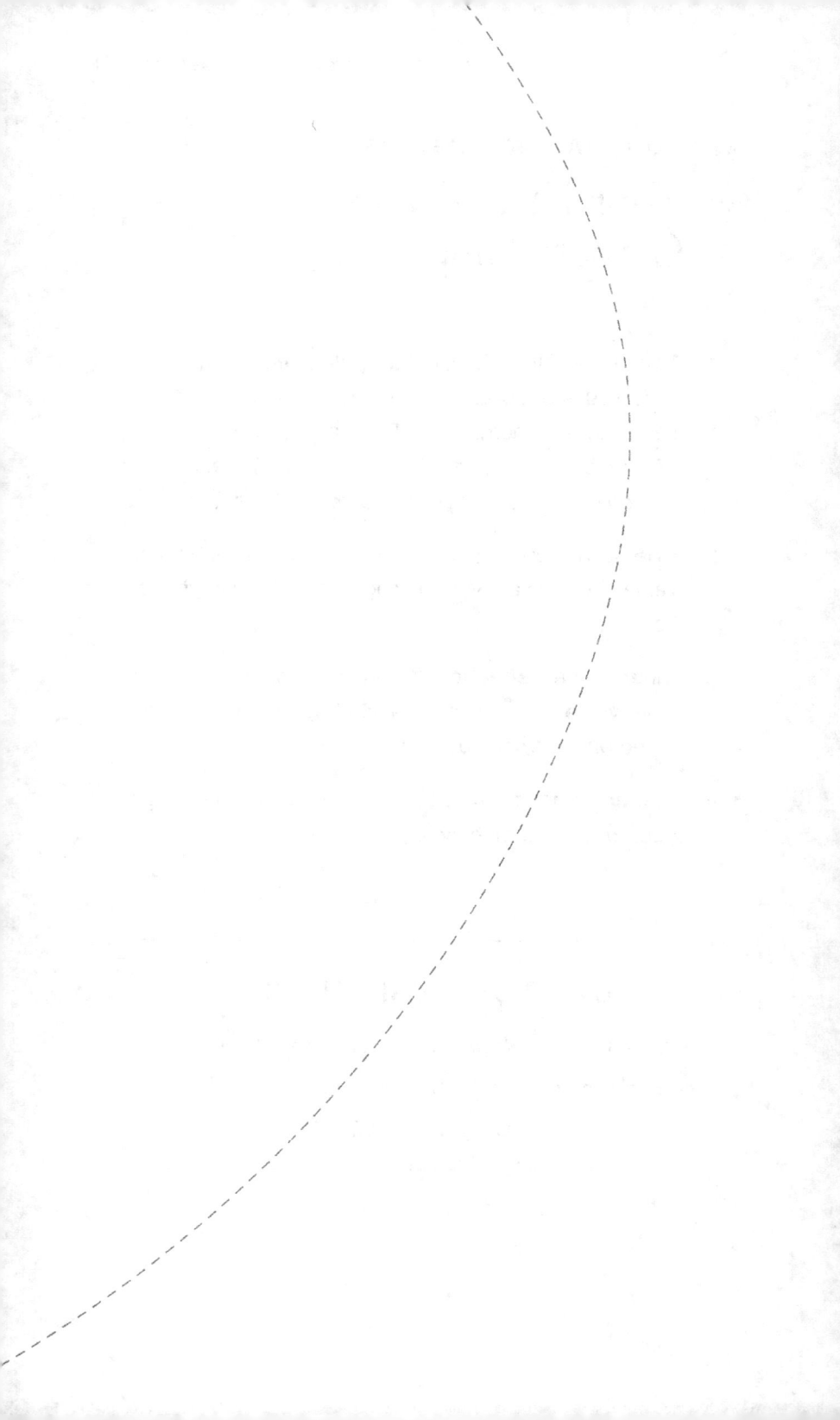

PUT THE CAR INTO YOUR CAREER

THROUGH MANY LEADERSHIP coaching conversations I have observed that many of my clients have a common bad habit—they put their job ahead of their career. When I ask, "Who is responsible for your career?" the answer is always a confident "I am!" But when I follow up with, "What are you doing about it?" I often see blank looks.

I love using analogies in my coaching conversations, and for this issue, I ask, "How do you spell career?" After they spell it out, I point out that the word begins with "car"—a subtle reminder that their career is like a vehicle that they need to drive. This simple observation reinforces the message that you must be in the driver's seat of your own career.

I ask my clients to visualize a basic four-passenger car as a representation of their career—with a driver's seat, a front passenger seat, and two back seats. Then I ask, "If this car were your career, which seat are you sitting in?" Believe it or not, only a couple of clients have said they are in the driver's seat. Most admit they are in the front passenger seat, and I have even had one client mention they were sitting in the back, looking out the rear window instead of facing forward. One client joked about feeling like they were stuck in the trunk.

This car analogy truly resonates with my clients, creating awareness that they need to proactively manage and steer their careers rather than remain passive. Many seem to be waiting for someone else to spontaneously notice their contributions and offer a new opportunity—a new assignment, a new job, or even a promotion. I love to see the lightbulb go off when clients declare that they are ready to take the wheel of their career. They begin to act by creating a future vision board, expanding their networks, exploring opportunities both internally and externally, and yes, updating their LinkedIn profile.

Corporations often offer a plethora of resources and events to help navigate careers. The key is for employees to realize that it's their responsibility to own their career—and to put their cars in drive.

JOURNALING EXERCISE
Get in the Driver's Seat

Imagine your career is a car. You are either driving it, riding along, sitting in the backseat—or, like my client, maybe even locked in the trunk. Where are you today—and where do you want to be?

Consider the following questions:

1. **Where Are You Sitting?** If your career were a car, what seat are you currently sitting in? How do you feel about this?

2. **Who (or What) Is Driving?** If you're not in the driver's seat, what forces, fears, or habits are steering your path instead?

3. **Taking the Wheel:** What is one action you can take this month to move into the driver's seat of your career?

4. **Creating Your Career Journey:** Imagine you are behind the wheel. Where do you want to drive your career next? What does that future road look like—and who or what will support you on the journey?

GENTLE REMINDER

No one else can drive your career but you. The road ahead is yours to create—turn the key, take the wheel, and choose your own direction.

COMMUNICATE YOUR AMBITION

ONE IMPORTANT LESSON I learned as a corporate leader—and now emphasize as a coach of emerging leaders—is the necessity of communicating your ambition. Many of my clients are eager to take on additional responsibilities or advance to the next level as they move through their career journey. Yet interestingly, many do not realize how important it is to express their aspirations.

A majority of my clients believe their manager—or higher-level leaders—instinctively know what's best for them . . . or worse, can somehow read their minds. Many hesitate to share their ambition, worried it might be misunderstood (as if they're unhappy where they are, for instance) or that speaking it aloud could invite unwanted judgment. Yet naming your ambition often opens doors to support, encouragement, and new opportunities. Being explicit about your goals, dreams, and aspirations is absolutely necessary. The only one who knows what is truly important to you or what you want to create in your future is *you*.

One client recently shared with her boss's boss that she would love an international assignment. To her surprise, the leadership team was thrilled to hear this. They had assumed—because she was married with young children— that she would never be open to relocating overseas for two years. By communicating her ambition clearly, she opened a door that leadership was eager to help her walk through. Interestingly, what she hadn't realized was that sending one of their top talents to the company's overseas headquarters would also signal the leadership team's commitment to succession planning—one of every large firm's most important HR processes.

Another story I love to share with my clients involves two talented women, Karen and Naomi. In my last corporate position, I led a large organization and spent much of my time getting to know the people on the team. One of my personal goals was to help them grow into the best leaders they could be.

Every year, we facilitated a talent review process, one focus being to identify successors for ourselves and for key leadership roles. Two men reported directly to me, and because their positions were critical to the organization's success, I was eager to identify strong successors. Karen and Naomi, both of whom reported to these leaders, were consistent high performers with exceptional leadership strengths. Naturally, I considered both for succession. As part of my preparation, I scheduled individual conversations with each woman.

When I met with Karen, I thanked her for her outstanding contributions and shared that I was considering her as a potential successor to her boss. I assumed she would be thrilled—after all, it would be a director-level promotion, a level to which many aspire. To my surprise, Karen quickly replied, "Whatever you do, please do not promote me."

She explained that she loved her current role, felt fulfilled by her responsibilities, and valued the balance she was able to maintain between her work and personal life. She didn't want to take on the additional demands that her boss's job would entail. I thanked her for her candor and once again expressed appreciation for her valuable contributions. It was a powerful lesson for me: I had made an assumption based on performance that wasn't aligned with her personal ambitions.

Later that afternoon, I met with Naomi. I had the same conversation with her—and her response was completely different. Naomi was elated. She said, "Yes, absolutely—I would love to be considered for a leadership role." She was transparent about her ambition and even shared that she aspired someday to be in my seat. I loved hearing that because her ambition was now clear—and it allowed me to find opportunities to help her grow. Three months later, when the VP of our Corporate Planning Office asked me to recommend top talent for an important initiative, Naomi immediately came to mind. I reached out to her with the opportunity, and she immediately accepted.

We transitioned Naomi from her current role to this new assignment, giving her the chance to develop in ways she would not have otherwise. And she did an outstanding job. Today, just five years later, she is a Senior Director and on track for even higher leadership roles, which she is thrilled about. Naomi's career trajectory might not have unfolded the way it did had she not clearly communicated her ambition and aspirations for growth. Communication is behind every success story.

JOURNALING EXERCISE

Owning and Communicating Your Ambition

Your ambitions are your own—but they can only be realized if you are willing to name them, own them, and communicate them with clarity. Today, reflect on how you can step more fully into your leadership journey by making your ambitions known.

1. **Clarifying My Ambition:** What is one goal, role, or opportunity you would love to pursue in the next few years?

2. **Naming Assumptions:** Have you been assuming that others (managers, mentors, leaders) already know what you want? What are you assuming they think? What might be possible if you shared your ambitions more explicitly?

3. **Facing the Fear:** What fears or hesitations come up when you think about communicating your ambitions? How might you reframe these fears as opportunities for growth, clarity, or connection?

4. **Taking a Small Step:** What is one conversation you can initiate this month to express your interests, goals, or aspirations to someone who can support your journey?

GENTLE REMINDER

*Leadership isn't just about waiting for the next opportunity—
it's about boldly naming the future you want to create and
inviting others to help you get there.*

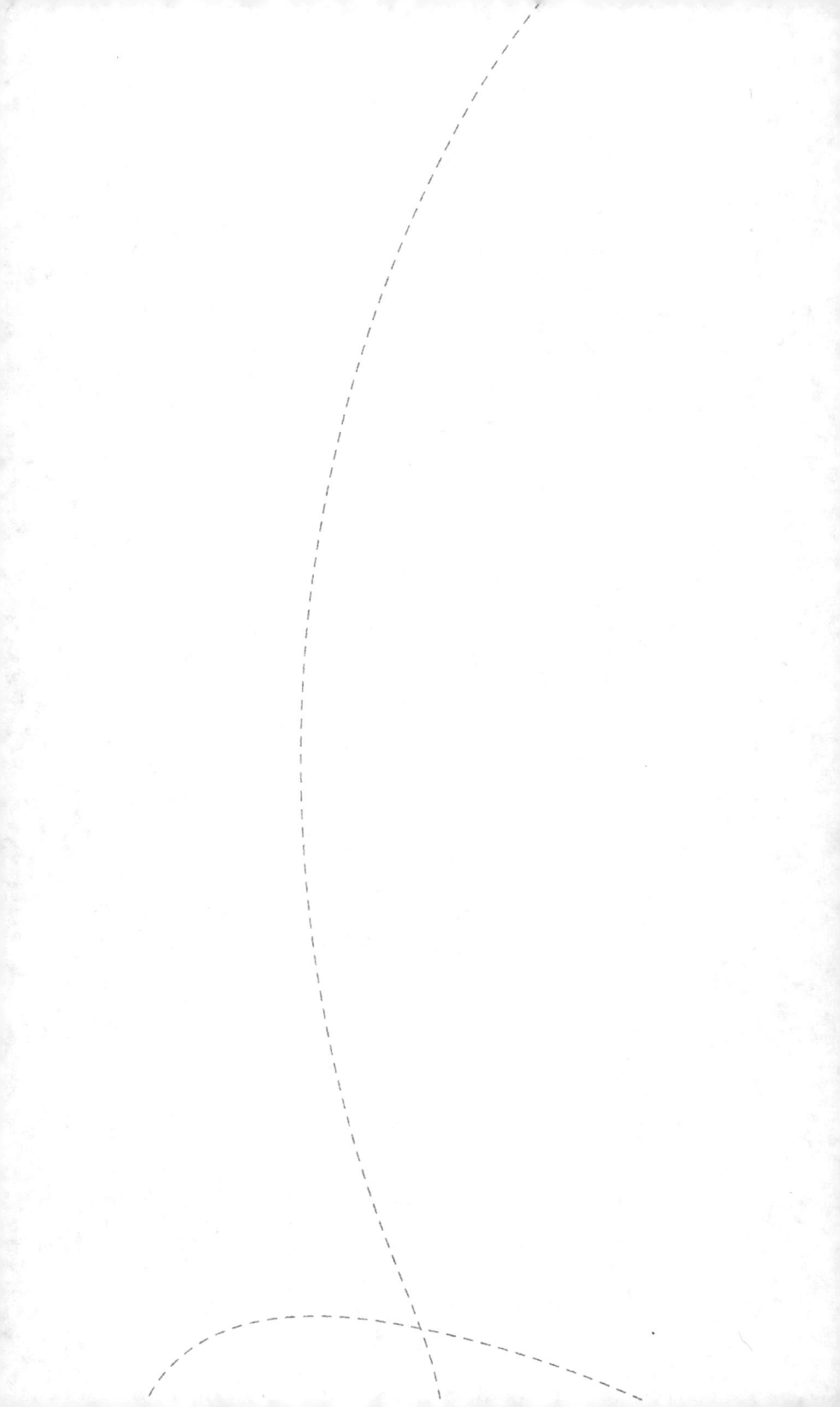

THIS IS WHAT REAL NETWORKING LOOKS LIKE

WHAT IS IT about the word *network* that turns people off? Many of my clients are quiet, reflective, and would consider themselves introverted, and when the topic of networking arises, they immediately cringe. It conjures up images of awkward mixers, transactional conversations, and the pressure to "sell" yourself—none of which feels authentic or energizing to them. They imagine crowded rooms filled with name tags and small talk, where genuine connection feels out of reach.

But what if we redefined networking as simply building relationships rooted in curiosity, generosity, and shared purpose?

As I mentioned earlier, I never took a single technology class in university. Yet in my career, I found myself leading and orchestrating technology teams—not because I could write code or architect systems, but because I could connect with people. While others focused on roadmaps and project plans, I focused on relationships. In a world driven by technology, it's the human connection that truly powers your career and propels your progress. I treated every interaction as an opportunity to build a bridge—long before I needed to cross it. Over time, those bridges became my greatest assets.

The human connection begins with simply being *human*. People bond at the human level. I often observed how frustrated people became when they weren't getting the results they needed from a conversation—and I'd realize they didn't really know the person they were talking to. They jumped straight into the agenda, skipping the *person* entirely. I know that I connected deeper with colleagues when I knew something personal about them—that they were also working parents, or lived nearby, or once attended a rival school, or shared a love of travel. Common threads make relationships stronger—and collaboration more effective.

A best practice I learned early on is to build your network before you need it. This idea has been widely studied and validated. Rob Cross is the Edward A. Madden Professor of Global Leadership at Babson College. He's an associate professor there and has studied organizational networks for decades and uncovered some fascinating patterns. In his research, he identified "fast movers"—relatively new employees who progressed quicker than longer-tenured leaders. What set them apart? When meeting new people, they didn't focus on selling themselves. They led with curiosity—asking thoughtful questions, seeking to understand the other person's priorities and challenges. And when they saw a way to help, they offered something of value. That act of generosity created trust and connection—and pulled them into new opportunities rather than pushing themselves forward.

I remember coaching a woman named Elena, a brilliant data scientist who dreaded any event labeled "networking." She once told me she'd rather spend an evening debugging code or cleaning her basement than attend a professional happy hour. But over time, we reframed her view. I encouraged her to see networking not as performance but as planting seeds: a chance to learn about others, share passions, and build relationships slowly, over time. One day when having coffee with a former colleague, she casually mentioned her interest in AI ethics. That simple conversation led to an unexpected opportunity—a speaking engagement that expanded her visibility and her confidence. And that one engagement led to more invitations, including a board role where she now shares her thought leadership on the topic.

When I started my coaching business, I experienced firsthand the power of a well-nurtured network. My connections and reputation allowed me to grow my client base faster than many other new coaches I knew at the time. By reaching out to a few trusted contacts through LinkedIn— people who were connected to my ideal clients—I was able to launch my business and establish a strong brand. For me, networking became a relationship dividend. It was a gift that kept giving, paying returns in unexpected and deeply meaningful ways long after the original investment of small talk and icebreakers.

And I've learned that some of the best returns come from the most unlikely places. I used to think of networking as a somewhat formal activity—something done at con- ferences, coffee meetings, or professional mixers. But over time, I've come to realize that real networking, the kind that sustains careers and shapes lives, often happens in far less polished places.

Like the barstools at the Gladstone Tavern.

The Tavern sits just down the road from where I live. It's a modern-day *Cheers*—a cozy place where everyone truly does know your name, and where community is served alongside cocktails. As a newly single woman after my divorce, I felt a little out of place navigating life on my own. But the Tavern quickly became a refuge. Every Tuesday night, a group of regulars gathers to "support" one of our favorite bartenders. I'm the only woman in this unofficial club, and I like to joke that I bring diversity to the group.

It's quite the cast of characters: a retired CFO, a bank executive, a general contractor, a former beltway insider, a local musician, an award-winning architect, a retired archeologist, a marketing wizard, and several entrepreneurs. Despite our differences, there's a shared respect, rhythm, and generosity of spirit. I didn't shape the group— but I showed up fully and confidently and was welcomed as one of their own.

One Tuesday night, a group of women wandered in and were clearly captivated by the chemistry and camaraderie they witnessed. They approached me and asked, "How do you become part of this group?" I smiled and said, "Well, I'm the secretary. All you need to do is write a $50 check to me and you're in." They laughed, spoke with the guys, and had a great time. At the end of the night, they asked for the spelling of my name so they could write the check. That's when I admitted it was a joke—there was no club, just real connection.

What I love most about this story of connection is how it blurs the line between social and professional networks. Many of those Tavern friends have introduced me to people in my industry, referred clients to my coaching practice, and offered support when I've needed it. And I've done the same in return. These aren't LinkedIn connections or CRM entries—they're real people who now know me, trust me, and want to help.

Leadership and networking aren't always about what you say in the boardroom—they're often about how you show up in the everyday. Your most valuable connections may be formed in unexpected places, with people who see you as human first. So, the secret isn't status—it's presence. Real relationships are built on consistency, authenticity, and a touch of humor. Whether you're sitting at a conference table or a barstool, showing up fully—curious, generous, and real—will take you farther than any business card ever could.

JOURNALING EXERCISE
Your Network Is Your Net Worth

1. **Think about a relationship in your life that started in an unexpected way—at a social gathering, through a neighbor, or at a casual meetup:**

    *   What drew you into that connection?
    *   How has it supported your personal or professional growth?
    *   How can you stay open to new, unconventional relationships that might enrich your leadership journey?

2. **Now take a moment to reflect on your current network:**

    *   Who are the people you trust the most right now?
    *   Are there any relationships you've been neglecting that you'd like to nurture?
    *   And who might you extend a hand to this week—no formal invitation required?

3. **Take some time to look to the future:**

    *   Imagine it's three years from now. What kinds of people do you want to be connected with—and why?
    *   What roles, opportunities, or circles would you like to be part of?
    *   What small step could you take this month to begin planting your seeds?

GENTLE REMINDER

Your network isn't built at big events—it's built in everyday moments. Forget the business cards. Real connection starts when you show up fully, stay curious, and engage like it matters. That's where leadership begins.

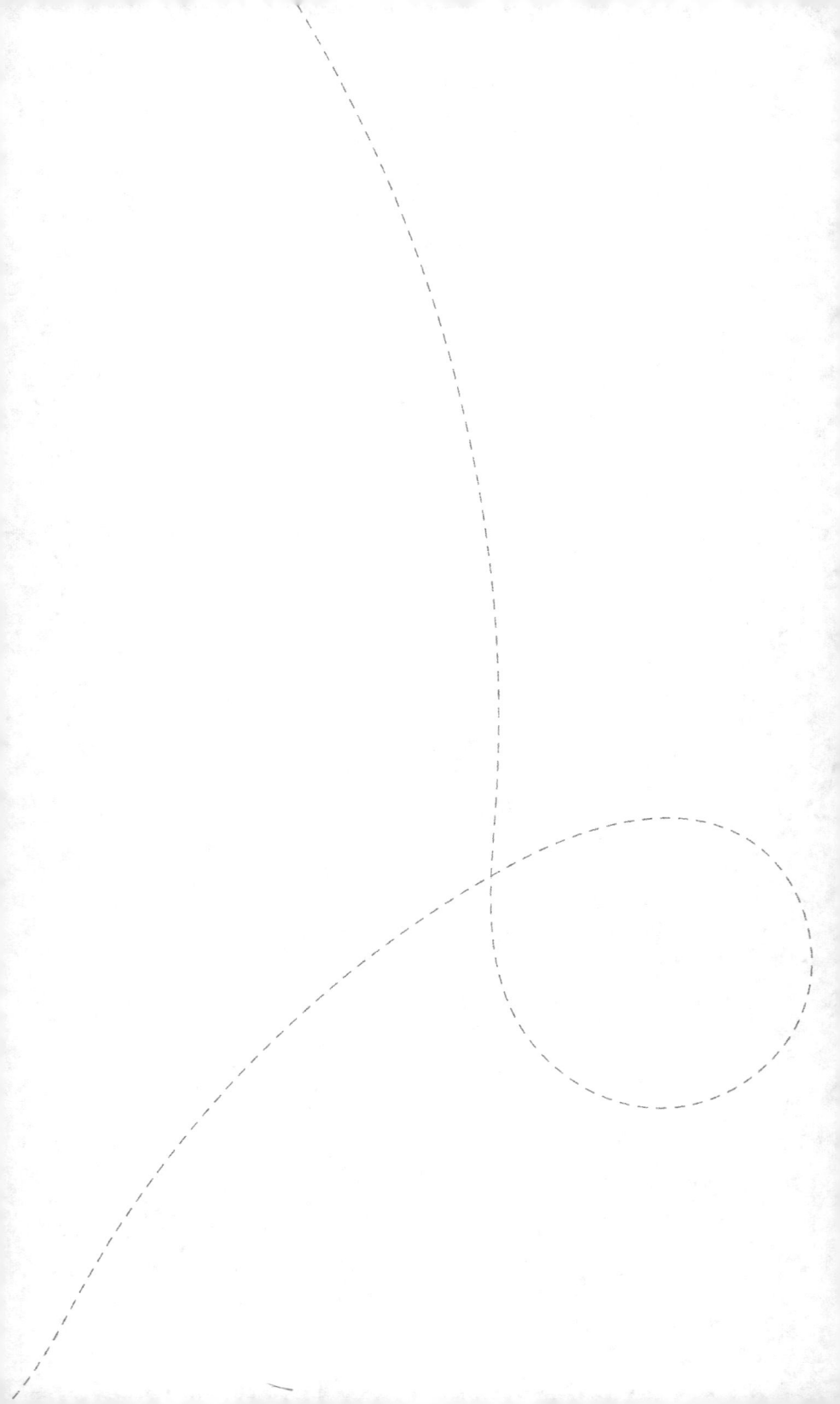

TEFLON SWEATER REQUIRED

The Art of Managing Stakeholders

NO ONE EVER taught me how to manage stakeholders. It wasn't part of a training program or in an official job description—though today, it's in almost every corporate job posting. I learned it the hard way: through experience. Over time, with lots of practice, difficult conversations, and more than a few character-building moments, I came to understand that managing stakeholders is one of the most essential leadership skills we can develop. Because the truth is, stakeholders are everywhere.

Let's start by defining the word *stakeholders*. They're not just people with formal authority; they're anyone who can influence your work or be affected by it. And navigating these relationships takes more than a status update or a polished slide deck. You need empathy, strategy, confidence—and the ability to show up without your ego. I often tell my clients: You've got to check your ego at the stake-holder's office door, whether that door is physical or virtual . . . or metaphorical.

Stakeholders typically listen through a filter of loss or gain—whether your message threatens something they care about, offers something they want, or gives them new respon-sibilities they didn't expect. If you don't understand their stance, it's easy to get blindsided by resistance or misaligned expectations. That's why I've learned to pause and ask:

- What matters most to this person?
- What's at stake for them?
- Where might they be feeling squeezed, stretched, or skeptical?

Let's get clear on what I mean by *stance*. A stakeholder's stance is their position—how they feel—about a given topic. There are five basic stances: strongly supportive, supportive, neutral, against, and strongly against. Your goal is to keep your stakeholders at least *supportive*, and ideally *strongly sup-portive*. *Neutral* is risky—it means they can easily be swayed to the *against* side.

To assess a stakeholder's stance, listen carefully during conversations. For example, if you share an idea and they respond, "That's a great idea—we've needed that for a long time," you know they're supportive. If they say, "I'm not really seeing how that could work," or "I have some issues and concerns about how we might implement that with limited resources," well, clearly you've got some work to do. Engaging *supportive* stakeholders is easy—the real work begins when you need to engage resistance.

And that's the heart of stakeholder management: engaging resistance. It requires inquiry more than advocacy. It's tempting to show up trying to persuade, convince, or explain. But the real power comes from listening—deeply— and asking the kinds of questions that invite openness.

One of my go-to reminders for clients is this: Open-ended questions are always your friend. When you are at a loss for what to say, you can always ask an open-ended question through a lens of curiosity. The best ones start with *What* or *How*. (Avoid *Why*—it tends to put people on the defensive, and that's the last place you want your stakeholder.)

I wasn't always good at this. Years ago, I remember being shocked when, in a steering committee meeting, a senior leader suddenly pushed back hard on something we had already aligned on—at least, I *thought* we had. In hindsight, I realized I'd relied on status updates instead of real conversations. I hadn't done the deeper listening. That experience taught me that influence doesn't come from having the best deck or argument. It comes from having the best understanding of the person across from you.

One of my clients, Celia, a senior IT director, learned this too. She was leading a high-stakes system rollout and assumed a key business leader was on board—until he derailed the project timeline in a leadership meeting. After regrouping, she and I walked through the stakeholder's stance together. Celia realized she'd never actually asked what mattered most to him or how the change might affect his team. She set up a 1:1 and went into it with a new goal: *listen first, solve later.* That conversation opened a new door—she learned he felt blindsided and overextended. By validating his concerns and co-creating next steps, she moved him from passive resistance to active support. It wasn't easy—but it was transformative.

And sometimes, when tensions rise, you need to wear what I call a Teflon sweater. When you're wearing a Teflon sweater, you're able to let the emotion or reactivity slide off you without taking it personally. That's the hardest part: staying grounded and curious when you'd rather defend or retreat.

When you master the art of stakeholder engagement, people begin to see you as a co-creator. They seek you out. They *want* to collaborate. This leadership skill is rooted in trust and influence—and it's what I call a life- and career-defining skill. Learn to manage stakeholders well, and it will serve you not only at work—but in every aspect of your life.

JOURNALING EXERCISE

Managing Stakeholders with Intention

Think of a project, relationship, or challenge you're currently navigating. Then reflect on the following prompts:

1. **Who are the key stakeholders?** Include both formal and informal influencers.

2. **What do you think their current stance is?**

   - Strongly Supportive
   - Supportive
   - Neutral
   - Against
   - Strongly Against

3. **What might be driving their stance?**

   - What do they stand to gain or lose?
   - What pressures or priorities might they be juggling?

4. **What open-ended questions could you ask them?** (Start with *What* or *How* to invite dialogue.)

5. **What part of your ego might need to be left at the door?** (Name it gently: needing to be right, needing approval, fear of rejection)

6. **What would it feel like to wear your "Teflon sweater" in this situation?** (How can you stay grounded, curious, and present—even in discomfort?)

GENTLE REMINDER

The strongest leaders aren't the ones with all the answers— they're the ones who ask the most thoughtful questions. Every stakeholder is a human being first. Approach them with curiosity, empathy, and a willingness to listen beyond the words. That's how trust is built—and how influence becomes lasting.

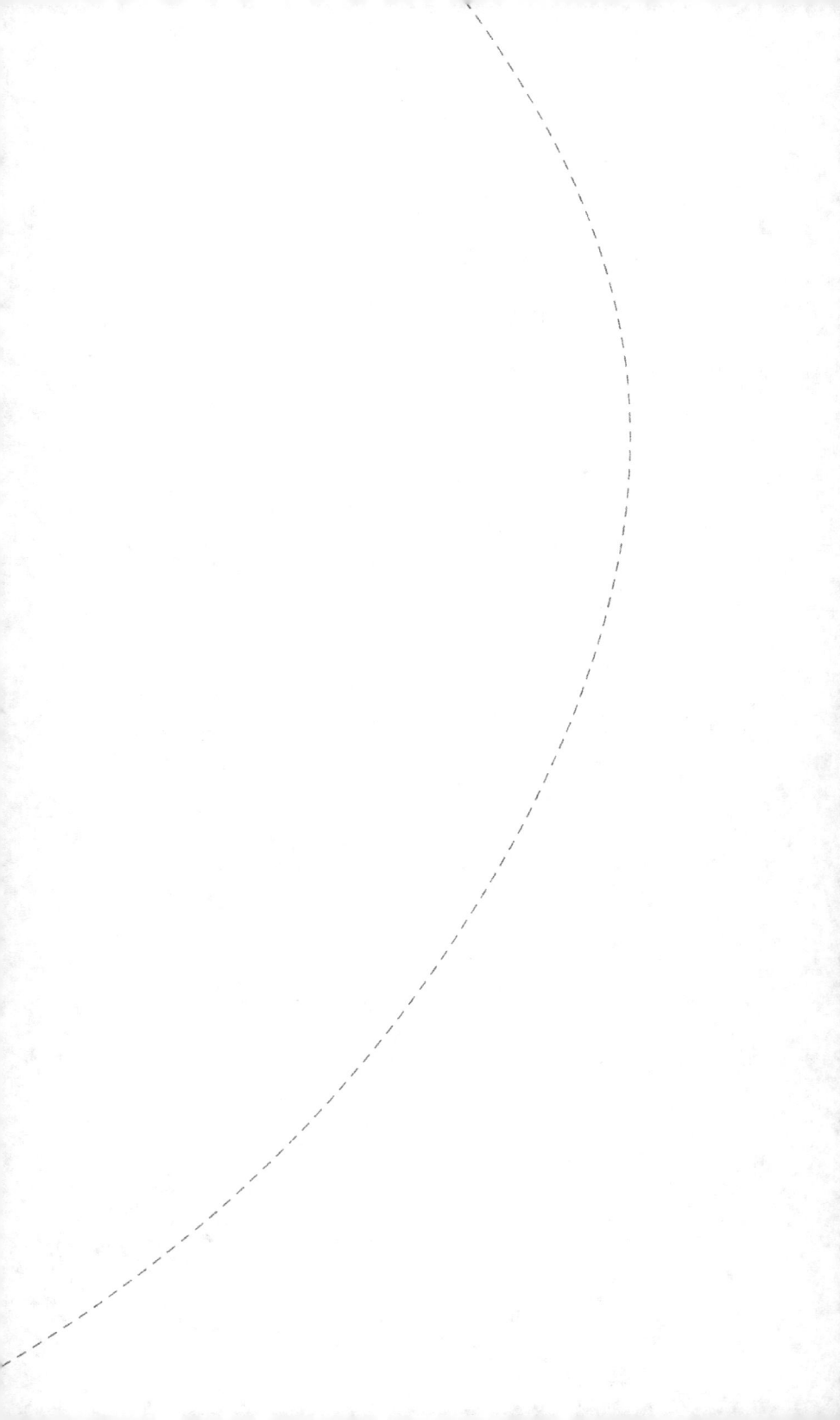

DON'T LET
THEM (OR YOU)
PIGEONHOLE YOU

BEING "PIGEONHOLED" IS something I have experienced personally and often discuss with my coaching clients. To be pigeonholed means you are seen as capable of only one specific role or set of tasks, making it challenging to explore new interests, take broader responsibilities, or transition into different fields. It's subtle yet restrictive—an invisible box that limits your growth and opportunities.

Early in my career at PerkinElmer, I found myself firmly pigeonholed. I was the Director of Marketing Communications, a prominent position with significant responsibilities. Leading a team of thirty talented professionals, I was successful in this role and genuinely enjoyed it. We achieved impressive results, and I was able to solidify my reputation as a dependable, organized leader skilled in communications and relationship-building.

After three years, however, I realized I was no longer learning or feeling challenged. I wanted to move beyond the boundaries of my role, perhaps into sales or a product management position. When I met with our company president to share this, his answer surprised me: a firm, immediate *no*. I vividly recall his exact words: "If I take you out of this position, who could ever do it as well as you?"

I felt deeply stuck, frustrated, and even confused. Did being good at my job mean I'd lost the right to evolve? Determined not to accept this fate, I requested he take additional time to reconsider. Two weeks later, his answer was unchanged. He believed I was irreplaceable in my current position, but that belief came at a cost. What he intended as praise felt like a firm limit placed upon my professional growth.

Despite the need for financial stability and knowing it was a risky move, I made the decision to step down. To mitigate the personal risk, I offered to stay on for five additional months to help hire my replacement and ensure a smooth transition. Honoring my desire to keep growing was imperative to me. My decision wasn't simply about leaving a job; it was about courageously kicking open the box I'd been placed in and reclaiming my potential.

True fulfillment comes from continuously redefining who we are and what we're capable of—especially when the world tries to neatly categorize us. Our careers should be full of pivots, reinventions, and exploration. Women, especially, owe it to ourselves to resist allowing others to limit our potential.

But here's a curveball, something else I've learned through years of coaching: Sometimes *we* are the ones who put ourselves in the box.

Many of my female clients don't just feel pigeonholed by their organization—they've also confined themselves to a version of who they think they're supposed to be. They describe the box they're in as safe, predictable, and even comfortable. They're good at what they do, they're valued, and they've built credibility. But many admit to me that inside, there's a quiet longing for something more—a bigger voice, more influence, a greater stretch.

When I hear this, I ask a simple but powerful question: What would it take for you to see yourself outside the box? They always have an answer. Sometimes it's more confidence. Sometimes it's feeling empowered to speak up, take a risk, or ask for what they really want. And that's where the coaching begins.

One client, a rising IT leader, told me, "I don't even know what I want next. I just know it's not this." We spent weeks exploring her strengths, values, and aspirations—not through the lens of her current job, but through the lens of her untapped potential. By the end of our engagement, she had a new role in a global function, a stronger voice at the table, and a renewed sense of self. And most important? There was no more talk of boxes.

Whether imposed by others or constructed by ourselves, boxes keep us small. And while stepping out of them can feel scary, it's also where growth, possibility, and leadership are allowed to live.

JOURNALING EXERCISE
Reclaiming Your Potential

1. **Identify the Box:**

   - In what ways might you be pigeonholed—either by others or by your own assumptions about who you are or what you're capable of?
   - What role, label, or expectation are you currently adhering to that may no longer serve your growth?

2. **Name the Longing:**

   - What part of you is quietly craving something more—more challenge, more purpose, more voice, more creativity?
   - What have you been hesitating to say out loud about what you really want next?

3. **Redefine Possibility:**

   - If there were no limitations—financial, professional, or personal—what kind of role, project, or path would you pursue?
   - What would it look like to step into a bigger version of yourself?

4. **Take a Small Risk:**

   - What is one bold yet simple action you could take this month to expand your possibilities? (Examples: initiate a new conversation, raise your hand for a stretch project, reach out to a mentor, enroll in a course)

- How would you support yourself emotionally and practically in taking that step?

5. **Write Your Future Bio:**

   - Write a short paragraph describing yourself three years from now, living outside the box. Use present tense. Who are you? What are you known for? What are you proud of? What have you let go of?

GENTLE REMINDER

You were never meant to be in a box. You're not limited to who you've been—or how others see you. Growth begins when you stop asking for permission and start trusting your potential.

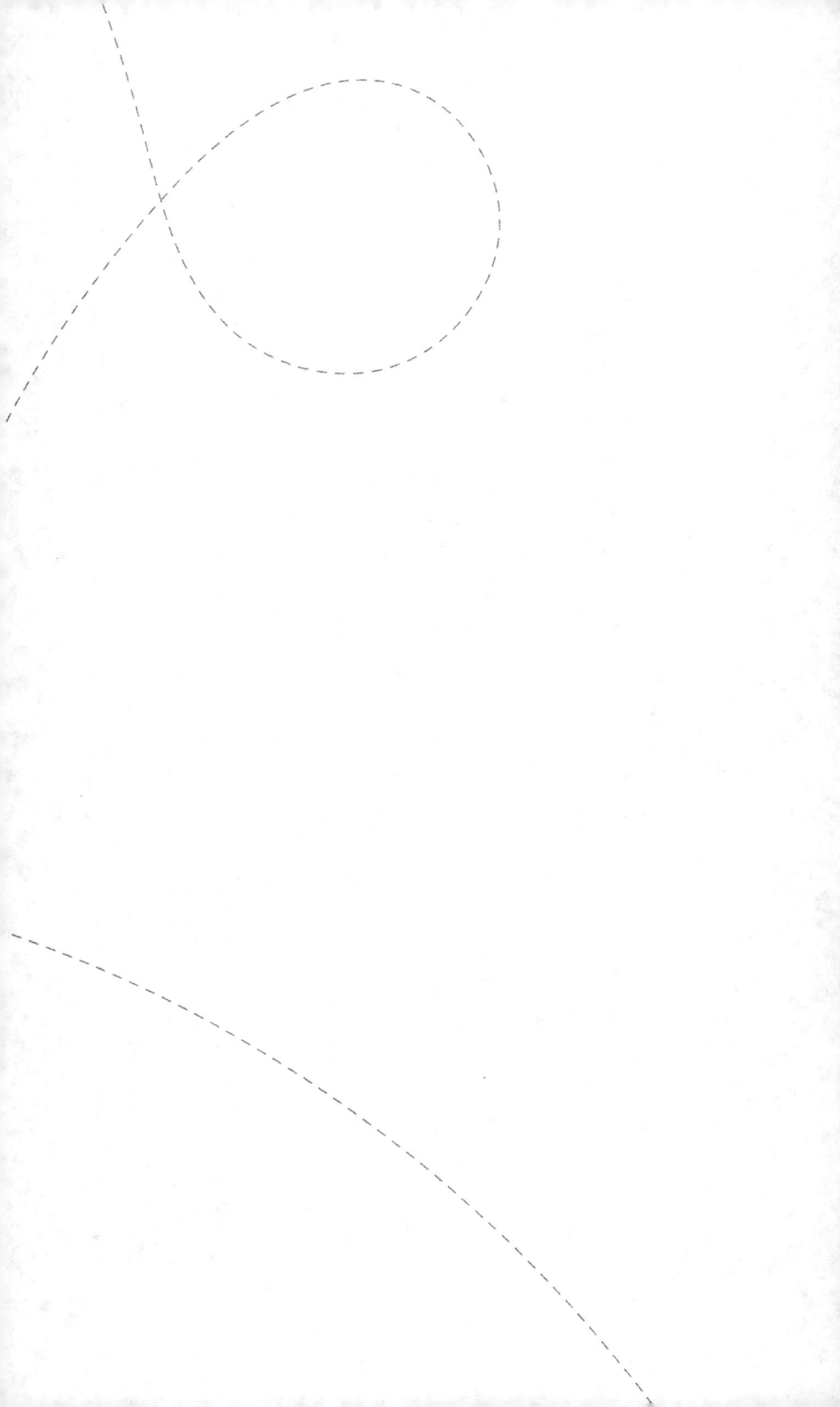

DISPELLING MYTHS OF CORPORATE LIFE

HAVING SPENT DECADES in large organizations, I've learned a lot—often the hard way. My aim is to help emerging leaders avoid unnecessary frustration and accelerate their growth. So when I became a leadership coach, one of my goals was to share what I call "the unspoken rules of corporate life," which often means shattering the myths that hold people back.

Many of my clients want to be promoted. They believe, quite reasonably, that their company tenure, hard work, long hours, and results should speak for themselves. But one of the first myths I like to challenge is that promotions are solely related to current job performance. They're also about perception and risk. When I ask my clients, "What do you think HR stands for?" they answer, "Human

Resources." That's when I smile and, with a touch of playfulness, offer an alternate definition: Human Risk. HR isn't in the business of promoting people on hope. They're in the business of managing human risk. They need to see and have confidence that you're already capable of operating at the next level.

I've lived this myself. When I was promoted to Executive Director at Merck, my boss showed up in my office one day and said, "We need to relevel your job—you're already working at the next level." Then he asked me to draft my own job description. That moment shattered another myth—that managers always define the job. In reality, shaping your own role is often part of the process. It's a great chance to advocate for the work you want to do—and minimize what doesn't energize you.

I've coached dozens of professionals stepping into director roles, and one recurring realization is that it's a much bigger leap than expected. One of my male clients had been promoted to being a new director a few months before our coaching engagement began. During our conversations, I realized he was doing the next-level job with his old shoes on. He hadn't fully realized that what made him successful previously was not enough to lead in this higher-level role. He needed to show up more strategically and with far more executive presence.

To mark this shift, I sometimes suggest that my clients envision a new pair of shoes—symbolic of stepping into greater responsibility. This client told me how much this metaphor meant to him. He would picture those bigger shoes before walking into any high-stakes meeting—and found it empowering. For my female clients, I often recommend a bold pair of red heels—a nod to confidence, visibility, and the strength they already possess.

Here's another common myth: Senior leaders already know what you know. That belief silences too many bright voices. One of my clients—a senior director working on a strategic digital initiative—was invited to a critical planning session with senior executives. She had deep expertise and valuable insights but stayed quiet, assuming others had already covered her points. Later, when she applied for a bigger role, she learned her silence had worked against her and, temporarily, held her back. It's a tough lesson: Your thinking doesn't count if it's not shared.

This reminds me of something Scott McNealy, co-founder of Sun Microsystems, once said. In my time at Sun, when people became a director, they were auto-matically enrolled in a new director training course. Scott personally kicked it off each time with a powerful main message: *Up to this point, your job was to have the answers. Now, your job is to ask the questions.*

It's an important shift. Asking great questions isn't just a skill—it's a leadership mindset. I often encourage my clients to trade in "expert mode" for "curiosity mode." Especially in meetings with senior leaders, showing up with curiosity—rather than a script—can change the entire dynamic. You don't need to dominate the conversation. You need to contribute, demonstrate strategic thinking, and invite dialogue by asking questions.

Open-ended questions are key. They open the door for real insight and engagement. I encourage clients to start small. Questions like, *What do you think? Where does this align—or not—with your thinking?* and *How do you feel about this direction?* are simple but powerful. The best questions start with *what* or *how*—and remember to avoid *why*, which can feel accusatory. Closed-ended questions tend to shut conversations down, whereas open-ended ones invite people into the conversation. That's where you want them.

Of course, this takes practice. Many of my clients return to our sessions saying, "That was harder than I expected." We're so used to leading with answers that it feels uncomfortable to pause and ask. But asking skillfully—especially in high-stakes meetings—is one of the strongest indicators of senior leadership presence.

Here's the bottom line: If you want to grow, you have to let go of outdated beliefs about how things "should" work. We often believe there's a simple effort-reward equation in corporate life. In actuality, it's a complex system of perceptions, relationships, and risk management. By learning how to shape your own path, speak up when it matters, and engage others through questions, you can lead with more confidence and insight—and fewer blind spots.

JOURNALING EXERCISE
From Insight to Influence

1. **Reflect on the Present:** Think about your last two or three meetings with senior leaders or cross-functional teams.

   - When did you speak up?
   - When did you hold back?
   - What was the impact in each case?

2. **Identify Patterns:** What beliefs or assumptions might be influencing your decision to stay quiet or speak up? (Examples: *They already know this, It's not my place,* or *I need to have a perfect answer.*)

3. **Prepare for the Future:** Write down three open-ended questions you can use in upcoming meetings to encourage dialogue, demonstrate strategic thinking, or engage key stakeholders. (Examples: *What's the biggest risk we're not seeing? How do you picture this aligning with our broader goals? What would success look like three months from now?*)

1. **Set a Micro-Goal:** Identify one upcoming meeting in which you'll practice asking at least one open-ended question. Write it here:

   Meeting: _____

   Question I'll ask: _____

   _____

GENTLE REMINDER

Growth means letting go of old myths and old shoes. Step into the role you aspire to with curiosity, courage, and presence—and others will soon see you already belong there.

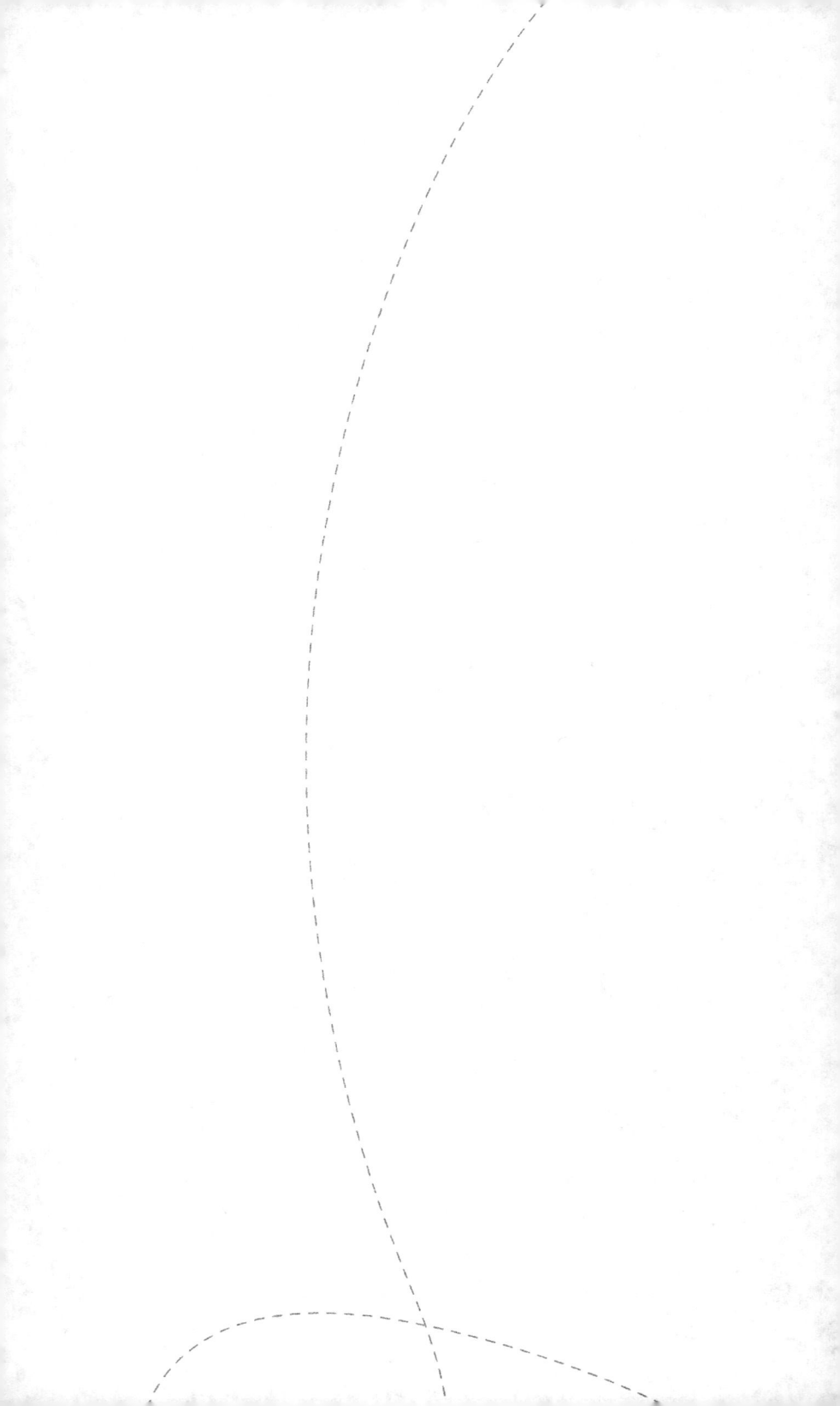

YOU AND YOUR CALENDAR

Who's Working for Whom?

TIME MANAGEMENT IS a topic I speak about with nearly all my clients. Many share that they feel overwhelmed, unable to accomplish their goals or complete their tasks. They confide that they are not focusing on the more important, strategic work—the very work that could help advance their careers. Instead, they're caught in endless meetings, with little time left for deep thinking, creativity, or self-care. They're stressed—and guilty (especially the women)—about spending too much time at work and not enough with their families.

A few years ago, one of my senior director clients came to her first coaching session after receiving feedback from her boss, who told her she needed to work more strategically. In these cases, I love to ask a simple question: How are you spending your time? Most clients pause before respond-ing, "I don't know."

Then I remind them that there are 168 hours in a week. No more, no less. Time is finite. You can't buy more of it. Once it's spent, it's gone. So, the real question becomes: How do you *want* to spend your time?

Many of my clients are what most would call worka-holics, logging fifty to sixty hours a week—sometimes even eighty. My role as a coach isn't to judge. It's to help create awareness so they can make conscious, empowering choices about their time.

Another question I love to ask is, "What is a calendar?" They usually look at me strangely before answering something like, "A tool for managing my time." And that's when I offer the real game-changer question: "Is your calendar working for you—or are you working for it?" This question always triggers an *a-ha* moment. They begin to see that their calendar is running them, not the other way around.

That same senior director returned to our next coaching session and announced: "I'm in all the wrong meetings!" She had done a calendar assessment and realized how much time she was spending reacting instead of leading. From that point forward, she started declining meetings, delegat-ing more, and proactively scheduling strategic conversa-tions with business partners—the very ones missing from her calendar before. A year later, she was promoted to VP.

Calendar management involves more than staying organized. It's about maximizing the return on your most precious resource: time. Yet many emerging leaders are hesitant to block time for themselves. They feel they should always be available, as if visibility equals value. Good leadership requires setting boundaries and sticking to them. I once had a boss who left work every day at 3:30 p.m. to go home and read. His role required him to stay current on research and innovation, but the office was full of interruptions. He protected that time to ensure success in his strategic role.

When my daughter was young, I made it a priority to drive her to and from school each day. That time with her was non-negotiable. I blocked it on my calendar and protected it fiercely. Today, wellness is one of my top priorities. I work out with my personal trainer three times a week—and that time is blocked like gold. Because it is.

Another calendar trap I often see is meeting overload. Clients accept every invite that comes their way—afraid to decline, fearing they'll miss something or disappoint someone. There's a reason why every meeting invitation has an option for declining; it's because you can. Some clients allow themselves to be double- or triple-booked. I recall when this started happening to me years ago. One day, I looked at my calendar, sighed, and asked my team, "Where's the cloning machine?" We laughed, and I made a declaration: "Until I clone myself, I'm done double-booking."

Recurring meetings are another quiet thief of time. At the start of any new initiative, someone sends out recurring invites, and—without much thought—we accept them. At first, our presence *is* needed. But as the work progresses, our role shifts. Too often, we keep showing up, even when we're no longer essential. These meetings can become what I call a "silent drag"—quietly consuming our attention while delivering little value. So, I developed a habit. Twice a year, I did a full calendar sweep. Of each meeting, I asked myself: Is this still the best use of my time? If not, I'd send a friendly note along the lines of, "I'm stepping back for now—but if you need me, just reach out." This simple practice gave me back many hours for focus and renewed energy.

One important lesson I learned was not to set the expectation that you'll attend . . . and then fail to show up. That erodes trust. It's far better to decline up front—and offer to contribute in another way, like sharing input in advance or following up later.

So, I present you with this important question: Is your calendar working for you—or are you working for it?

JOURNALING EXERCISE
Taking Control of Your Calendar

Look Back:

- What do the last two weeks of your calendar say about your priorities?
- Which meetings truly needed you—and which didn't?
- How has over-calendaring impacted your personal priorities and what regret has that caused?

Look Ahead:

- Imagine your ideal calendar six months from now. What's on it?
- What boundaries have you set?
- What one small change can you make this week to move toward that vision?

GENTLE REMINDER

Your calendar is more than a scheduling tool— it's a reflection of your values, focus, and leadership. When you take ownership of your time, you signal to others what truly matters. Protecting your time isn't selfish—it's a powerful act of intentional leadership.

PART IV

Leadership from the Inside Out

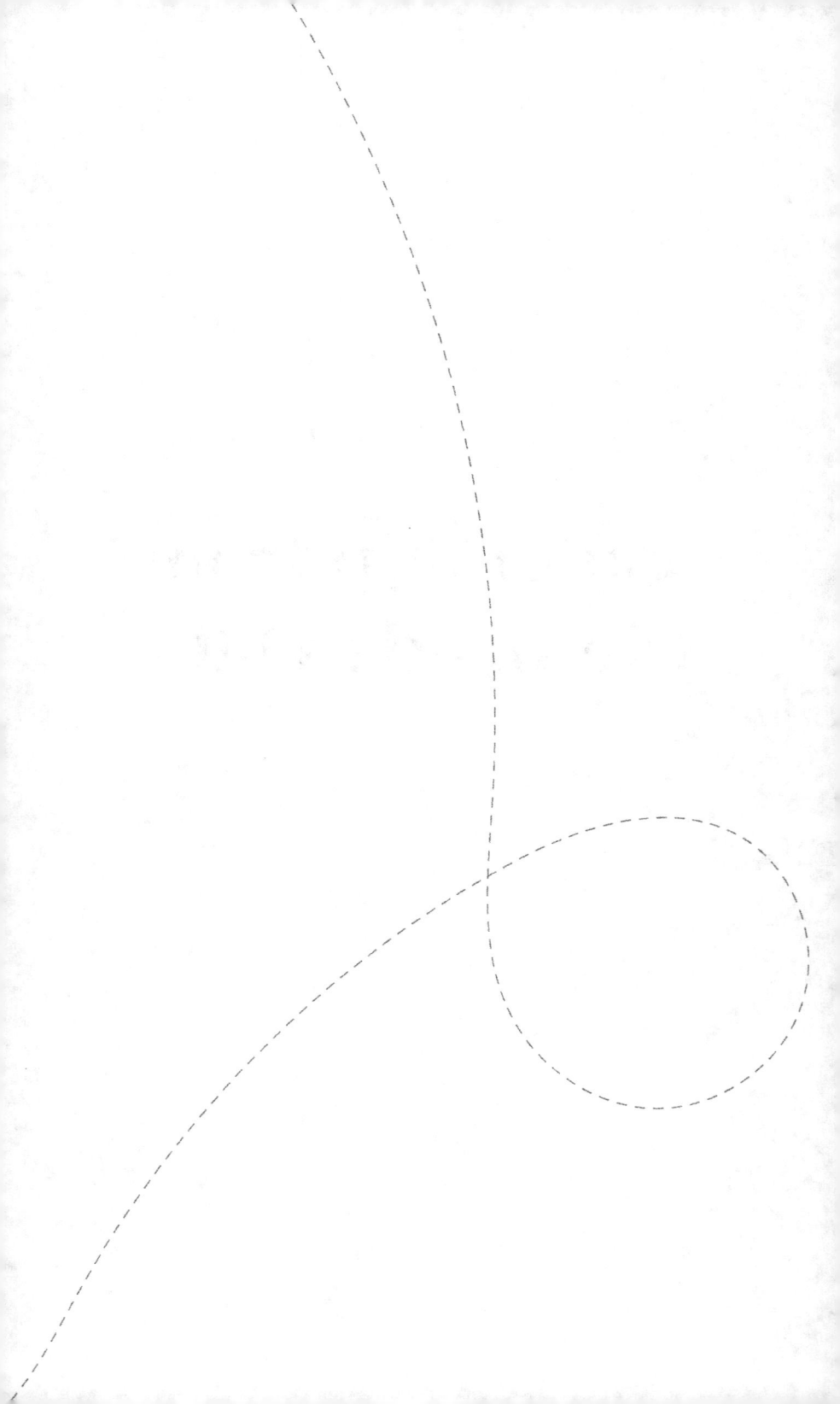

DOING VERSUS BEING

WHEN I'M ASKED how I define leadership, my answer is simple. To me, leadership is about two words—*Doing* and *Being*.

When I introduce this concept to my clients in Zoom sessions, I often use their collaborative whiteboard feature. I draw a Venn diagram—two circles to show that Doing and Being are two distinct aspects of leadership, and yet they overlap—because there is only one of you.

- The Doing circle represents what leaders do—tasks, decisions, actions.
- The Being circle represents who leaders be—character, presence, essence.

Yes, the poor grammar is intentional. It's not about who leaders *are*—it's about *who they be*.

To explain the distinction, I lead a simple exercise that usually takes five to ten minutes. I ask my client to think of a leader they admire—someone from work, outside of work, or in their community. Once they have someone in mind, I invite them to quickly name five characteristics of that person. As they speak, I jot the words down on the whiteboard. Some of the words that often emerge from this exercise are approachable, authentic, direct, truthful, compassionate, empathetic, consistent, empowering, courageous, and integrity-driven.

Next, I ask them to think of a leader they do *not* admire—and again name five characteristics, which I add to the list. Some of the words that emerge this time are aloof, micromanaging, egotistical, spiteful, lacking empathy, accusatory, shallow, and illusive.

When we have ten characteristics, I guide them through sorting each trait into the appropriate circle—Doing or Being. What's fascinating is that, in the hundreds of times I've done this exercise, the results have been remarkably consistent: About 75 to 80 percent of the leadership characteristics fall into the *Being* circle.

So, what does this tell us? It underscores how important a leader's *Being* is. It's not just about what they do—it's in large part about who they be. In the words of the poet Maya Angelou, "People will forget what you said, people will forget what you did, but people will never forget how you made them feel."

In my last position, when I was leading a large function, I was highly intentional about focusing on my Being. I literally wrote down the words I wanted to embody as a leader. I believed that doing so would give me crystal clarity—and allow me to live those words in every interaction.

My goal was simple. If someone I know one day participates in a Doing-vs-Being exercise and thinks of me as an example, what words would I want them to say? The words I chose were: approachable, honest, fair, compassionate, trustworthy, and respectful. Every day, I looked at these words and challenged myself: How am I living into these words today? How am I showing up in a way that reflects who I want to be?

One word stands out vividly even now, ten years later: approachable. When I first set the intention to be more approachable, I realized a small but important habit I needed to change. I couldn't continue to walk through the hallways looking down at my phone. I needed to make eye contact, smile, and greet people warmly. So, I started putting my phone in my pocket, lifting my head, making eye contact, waving, and saying hello—simple acts that created a sense of openness and connection.

It became a daily practice of Being—not just Doing. I became truly focused on embodying my leadership. This required me to integrate what I was thinking in my mind, with my body and my emotions. I focused on my nonverbal cues—like body language and gestures—in addition to my words. I increased my awareness of how significantly these contributed to my ability to communicate and influence.

To connect my thoughts with my physical presence and emotional intelligence required a higher level of self-awareness than I'd ever achieved before. And the result was outstanding. I was fundamentally able to shape how others experienced me and my leadership.

JOURNALING EXERCISE
Embodying Your Leadership

1. **Today's Awareness:** Choose three words that reflect how you *want* to show up as a leader today and write them down. At the end of the day, reflect:

   - *In what ways have I embodied these qualities today?*
   - *Where did I fall short, and what might have gotten in the way?*

2. **Tomorrow's Intention:** Looking ahead, pick one of those words you want to embody next week more fully and answer the following:

   - *What does this quality look like in action?*
   - *What specific situation or interaction could be an opportunity to practice it?*
   - *What's one small habit shift (like putting my phone away, smiling, or slowing down) that could help me live it more fully?*

GENTLE REMINDER

Leadership is more than what you do—it's how you show up. Each day is a chance to align your actions with your intention. Ask yourself: Am I being the leader I want others to experience?

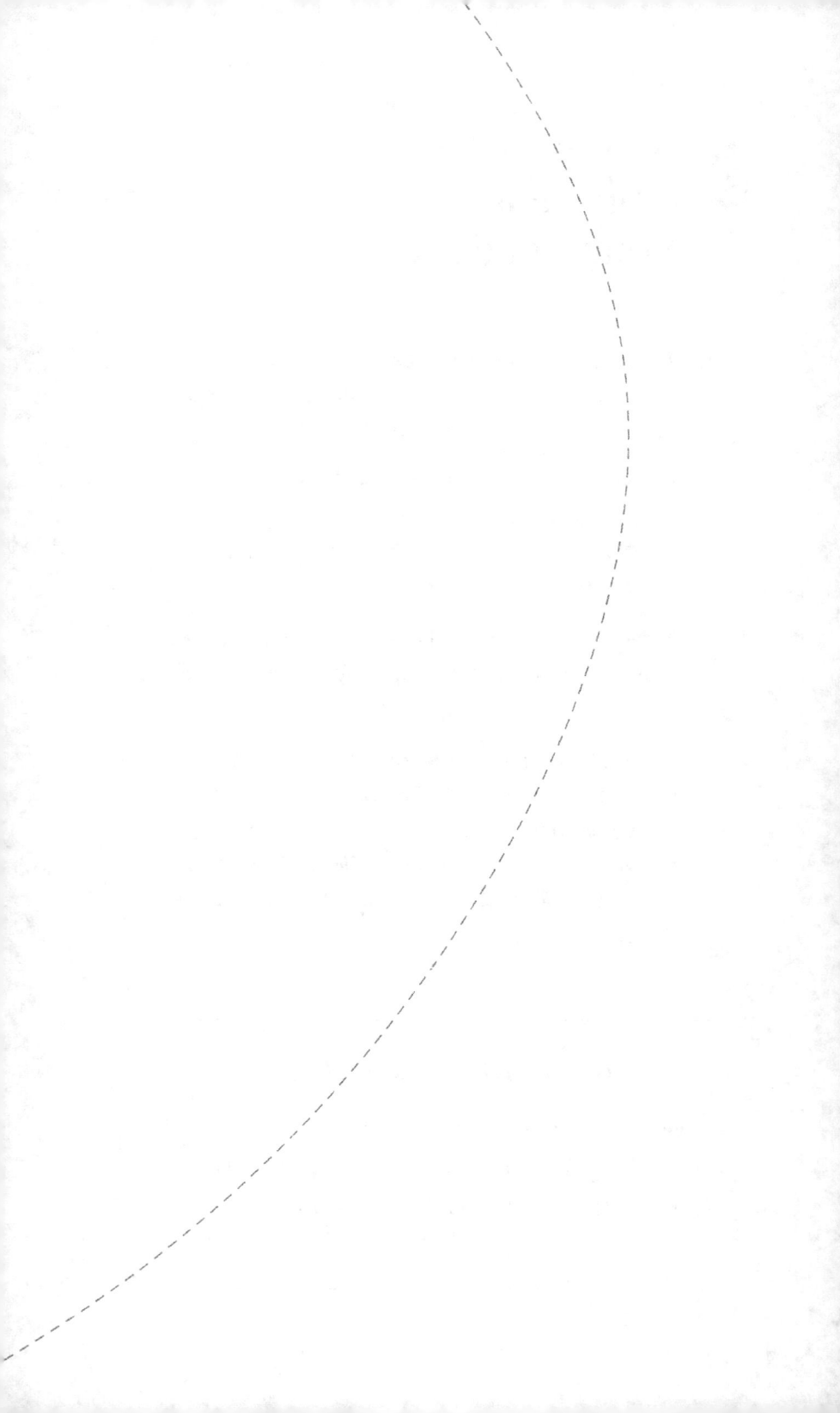

UP THE LADDER WITHOUT A CLUE

IT'S AMAZING HOW fast we can convince ourselves something is true—with nothing more than a glance, a gut feeling, and an old belief we've never questioned.

We all have an inner critic—that voice in our head that whispers (or sometimes shouts) self-doubt, judgment, and fear. It's part of being human. No one is immune to it, no matter how confident, accomplished, or self-aware they may seem on the outside.

This story is about one simple framework that changed the way I lead and live: the *Ladder of Inference*. The first time I encountered the Ladder of Inference was during an organizational change management class at Sun Microsystems. This deceptively simple model was developed by organizational psychologist Chris Argyris, a former Yale and Harvard professor who spent much of his career exploring why smart, capable people often struggle to learn from their experiences—especially in high-pressure environments.

It felt like someone had just handed me a flashlight for my brain. I didn't just learn about the Ladder of Inference—I was living it.

What Argyris noticed was something we all do: Observe a situation, quickly make meaning of it, and act—all in a matter of seconds. The problem? Most of the time, we aren't even aware we've made that mental leap.

While our inner critic may sound convincing, research and experience suggest it's wrong far more often than it's right—some psychologists estimate it gets things wrong up to 80 percent of the time. That's because our inner voice doesn't speak from fact; it speaks from fear, assumptions, and potentially outdated beliefs. We climb the ladder so quickly it becomes a mental shortcut. Instead of pausing to check what's actually true or possible, we fill in the blanks with old stories and faulty conclusions. The more we believe the inner critic, the higher we climb on the Ladder of Inference—and the further we get from the base of reality.

Argyris designed the Ladder to help us *see* this invisible thought process. Step by step, it reveals how we go from raw data to assumptions, to beliefs, and then to action—often skipping the possibility that our starting point might be incomplete or biased. The goal of the Ladder isn't to slow us down but to wake us up. It gives us a way to reflect on how our thinking shapes our actions—and how different our choices might be if we paused, even briefly, to question the stories we're telling ourselves.

Everyone on the planet has their own ladder. I tease some clients about having extension ladders! And many times, the ineffectiveness of conversations comes from the fact that both people are climbing their ladders at the same time. Heated conversations, especially, are often not based on current fact but on misinterpretation and history-driven inference.

Once I became aware of the Ladder, I began to recognize how some of my old beliefs were no longer serving me. I also could see how fast I was leaping to con-clusions—at work and in my personal life.

For instance, a few years after my divorce, I started dating again. I met a man online for lunch and really enjoyed his company. I found him worldly, smart, interest-ing, and engaging. After lunch, I was looking forward to seeing him again. Several days went by, and he never called or texted. I assumed he wasn't interested and felt a little sad about it.

When my daughter asked if I had heard from him, I said no. She asked, "Well, did you reach out to him?" I replied, "I couldn't. Women shouldn't call men first." And as soon as I said it out loud, I realized my bias. *That's an old belief—and it's not serving me anymore.* After reflecting for another day, I decided to text him. That simple message led to another date, and we ended up casually dating for a couple of years. I enjoyed the relationship and was so glad I challenged myself and tried a new approach.

As a coach, I hear my clients making inferences all the time. During our sessions, they often describe situations they want to change, and as I listen, I usually hear more interpretation than fact. When this happens, I ask for permission to share the Ladder of Inference with them—and teach them how it works. I then watch while the proverbial light bulb clicks on, as if I've handed them the same flashlight I received years ago.

Once they learn the Ladder, I share a simple way to step off it: Ask yourself, *What are the facts of this situation?* I've observed that nine times out of ten, there are no more than one or two facts in the twenty minutes of context they've just provided.

Clients tell me the Ladder of Inference has enriched their lives. Many have taught it to their teams, and one client even shared that she taught it to her husband and daughters and posted a picture of it on her kitchen refrigerator. It reminds everyone to stay focused on facts.

Consider embracing another powerful action: Because we all have inference ladders, start to listen differently when others speak. Try to discern whether their discussion points are grounded in facts—or whether they're climbing their Ladder. If so, you might gently help them down by returning to the core truths of the situation.

This kind of self-awareness makes you not only a more effective communicator and leader—but also a more grounded and compassionate human being. The more aware we become of the stories we tell ourselves, the more space we create to rewrite them—with clarity, compassion, and truth.

JOURNALING EXERCISE

Fact or Inference?

1. **Think of a recent situation in which you felt frustrated, hurt, or misunderstood.** Write a short description of what happened.

2. **Now ask yourself: What are the facts of the situation?** List only what is objectively true—no interpretations, no assumptions.

3. **Reflect on the story you told yourself.** What beliefs, assumptions, or fears were driving your interpretation?

4. **How might your actions or feelings have been different if you had paused to ask, *What are the facts?***

5. **What is one outdated belief you're ready to let go?** Write it down. Then, write a new belief to replace it— one that serves the person you are becoming.

GENTLE REMINDER

Your inner critic may speak loudly, but it doesn't always speak the truth. Each time you pause to check the facts, you reclaim your power—and open the door to a wiser, more compassionate way forward.

THERE IS ONLY ONE OF YOU

MANY LEADERSHIP ARTICLES and books have been written on the topic of authentic leadership. Authentic leadership is about leading from the inside out—while being grounded in self-awareness, guided by core values, and committed to being genuine regardless of the situation. Authentic leaders typically lead with integrity, vulnerability, and purpose. They build trust through their actions and not just their words. In my own leadership journey, I've found that the most powerful moments—both mine and those I've witnessed in others—have come from this place of being authentic.

This is a topic I discuss with most of my clients. It's always interesting to listen to them describe themselves—it's as if there are three or four versions of them. A woman I coached once described herself as if there was a professional version, a home (mother/wife) version, a community version, and a social friendly version of herself. I remember sharing my observation. "Wow! It sounds like there are four of you! That sounds complicated. What if there could be just one of you?" She smiled, acknowledged my observation, and asked, "How can I do that?"

That's when I introduced her to the concept of being an authentic leader. I explained that authentic leaders don't wear masks or play roles. They bring their whole self to every situation—whether it be at work, as a mom, or with friends. Many women I coach have the feeling that they need to put on a professional face at work to be taken seriously. My sense is that this comes from a place of insecurity and not feeling confident with themselves. It may also be rooted in a previous experience that didn't go well, leaving them leery now.

When someone is authentic, they can just show up and be. I love to share Bill George's powerful metaphor to describe authentic leadership. In his book, *True North*, he invites us to imagine a house with four rooms: the head (intellect and logic), the heart (emotions and compassion), the gut (instinct and courage), and the spirit (values and purpose). He writes, "Most people live in one or two rooms most of the time, but authentic leaders tear down the walls between the rooms and live in all four all the time."

My clients find this metaphor inspirational, and many agree to identify an action they can practice immediately. A brilliant data scientist I coached realized how much time she wasted rehearsing and scripting for every conversation she had at work. She also realized that her presence had become robotic instead of authentic. She was even thrown off when she was asked a question she hadn't thought of in advance. Her lack of authenticity was causing her to work longer hours, diminishing her confidence, and not allowing her brilliance to shine through.

Over time—with more and more practice and less rehearsing—she began to trust herself. She realized that no one knew her content better than she did. One day she was called into an unexpected meeting with the VP of her organization. She'd had no advance preparation, but even without her notes and well-prepared PowerPoint deck, she wound up having an amazing conversation—offered her expertise, shared her perspective, and answered all his questions with authority. She had been fully authentic.

That day turned out to be a huge boost for her confidence and the beginning of her true self showing up. Several conversations later, she shared with me how much time she was saving by not having to overprepare. Authenticity isn't about playing a part—it's about having the courage to bring your whole self forward, and trust that being yourself is always enough.

JOURNALING EXERCISE

Bringing My Whole Self All the Time

Authentic leadership is about bringing your whole self forward with courage, clarity, and heart. Today, explore how you can tear down the walls between your "rooms" and show up as one powerful, authentic you.

Consider the following:

1. **The Rooms I Live In:** When you think about your life (work, home, community, friends), are there places where you feel you have to "split" yourself into different versions? What masks or roles do you sometimes feel pressured to wear?

2. **My True Self:** Remember a time or situation in which you felt most like yourself—free, confident, and real. What were you doing? How would you describe that version of yourself in a few words?

3. **Living in All Four Rooms:** Consider George's concept of four rooms—head (logic), heart (emotion), gut (courage), and spirit (values). Which room feels strongest for you right now? Which room might you want to reconnect with more intentionally?

4. **Practicing Wholeness:** What is one situation coming up where you could practice showing up with more of your whole self—when there could be less performing and more being?

GENTLE REMINDER

You are not meant to split yourself into pieces to fit the world. Your greatest power comes from bringing your full, beautiful, wise self forward—in every room, every role, every moment.

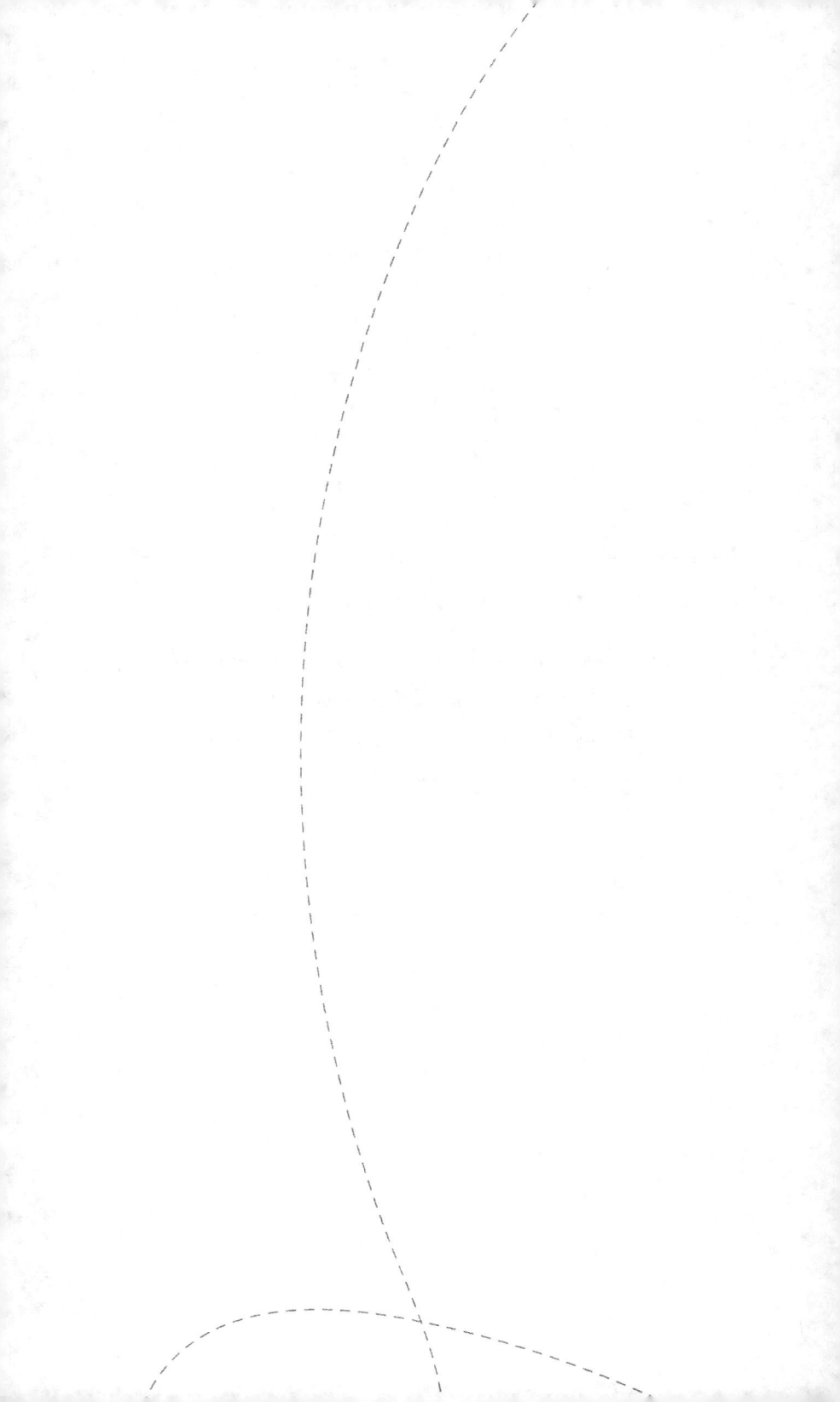

THE POWER OF KNOWING YOUR TOP FIVE

I'VE TAKEN JUST about every personality assessment out there—Myers-Briggs, Insights, DISC, you name it. Each one offered helpful insights, mostly about how I interact with others or how I might need to adapt in team settings. But the first time I took the StrengthsFinder 34 assessment— fifteen years ago—it was something entirely different.

It wasn't about how to fit in or flex for others. It was about *me*—just me.

The report stacked my thirty-four strengths in order, showing me a mirror I hadn't held before. And the most powerful part? My top five strengths formed a unique fingerprint—one that helped me understand my leadership DNA. The report also identified potential blind spots, which was critical because any strength, when overused, can become a weakness.

Since then, I've used this tool both as an organizational leader and with hundreds of clients in my coaching practice—and not once have I seen the same top five strengths repeated. That's how I know: StrengthsFinder 34 isn't just a report. It's a roadmap. And for many of us, it's the first step to unlocking our full potential—from the inside out.

What I've learned—and what I hear echoed by my clients—is that StrengthsFinder (now also known as Clifton-Strengths) gives us refined language to express our strengths, which in turn boosts our confidence. When you realize that the person sitting next to you doesn't share your top five, it becomes easier to recognize and articulate your unique contribution and the value you personally bring to any conversation.

In my corporate leadership roles, I attended many strategic planning sessions—sometimes day-long workshops involving multiple stakeholders. I remember those days clearly. We'd be brainstorming for hours, sticky notes covering the walls, energy high but often scattered. More than once, late in the afternoon, I'd find myself jumping up to the whiteboard, scanning the sea of ideas and saying something like, "What if we take this idea, combine it with this one, and link it to that over there? Together, they could lead us to a bigger outcome no one's named yet." People would look at me and say, "How did you see that?" And honestly, I didn't know.

StrengthsFinder later showed me that I had the strength of *Connectedness*—a less common strength that often shows up in people who are reflective, values-driven, and drawn to meaning or spirituality. Suddenly, I could name what I had always sensed. And interestingly, after I started talking about this strength out loud, I was invited to more of those types of meetings. I was seen—and valued—as someone who could make unique, unexpected connections.

Woo is another interesting strength—and one I rarely see in tech environments, especially among engineers, developers, or data scientists. People with Woo (which stands for *Winning Others Over*) are often the "people people" in a sea of task-oriented minds. They naturally build bridges, spark collaboration, and bring empathy into the room. In all my years, I've only met three people with Woo in their top five. One of them, my client Rhonda, worked in manufacturing and was a force of nature. She didn't just network—she connected on steroids. She built relationships across silos, creating influence and trust where others relied on hierarchy or technical expertise.

Over the past fifteen years, I've taken the Strengths-Finder assessment three times. While a couple of my top five strengths have stayed the same, others have shifted depending on the role I'm currently in. Recently, I retook the assessment to see how my strengths align with my work as a leadership coach. Here's my latest top five:

Maximizer, Ideation, Self-Assurance, Adaptability, and Futuristic.

Just for fun, I asked ChatGPT what roles best fit someone with these strengths. Two answers stood out—and spoke to exactly why I love the work I do:

Executive/Leadership Coach:

Why: You challenge people and systems to evolve (*Maximizer*), create customized paths to growth (*Ideation*), and inspire bold visions (*Futuristic*), all while adapting to each client in the moment (*Adaptability*).

...and...

Change Management or Transformation Leader:

Why: You confidently lead people into the unknown (*Self-Assurance*), see possibilities others don't (*Futuristic + Ideation*), and help teams not just cope with change, but optimize it (*Maximizer*).

This validation is powerful evidence of how our strengths shape who we are and how we show up in the world. They shape our choices, our roles, and the value we offer to the people and teams around us. It's a bit like the chicken and the egg. Which came first? Your strengths, or the work you were born to do?

JOURNALING EXERCISE
Your Strengths in Action

1. **Today's Awareness:** Look at your current top five strengths. (If you haven't taken the StrengthsFinder assessment yet, consider doing so or discover your strengths from another tool you trust.) Now, consider:

    *   Which strength feels most alive or visible in your day-to-day work right now?
    *   How is it helping you contribute or lead more effectively?
    *   Where might you be overusing this strength? How could it be misunderstood by others?

2. **Tomorrow's Intention:** Choose one strength you'd like to lean into more intentionally in the coming weeks. Then reflect on the following:

    *   What opportunities or situations would allow you to activate this strength more fully?
    *   How might using this strength open new doors—or shift how others see you?

GENTLE REMINDER

Your strengths are more than skills—they're the essence of how you lead, connect, and create impact. When you lead from your strengths, things feel more natural, more energizing, more you.

Pay attention to the strengths that show up with ease—they're pointing you toward your most authentic path.

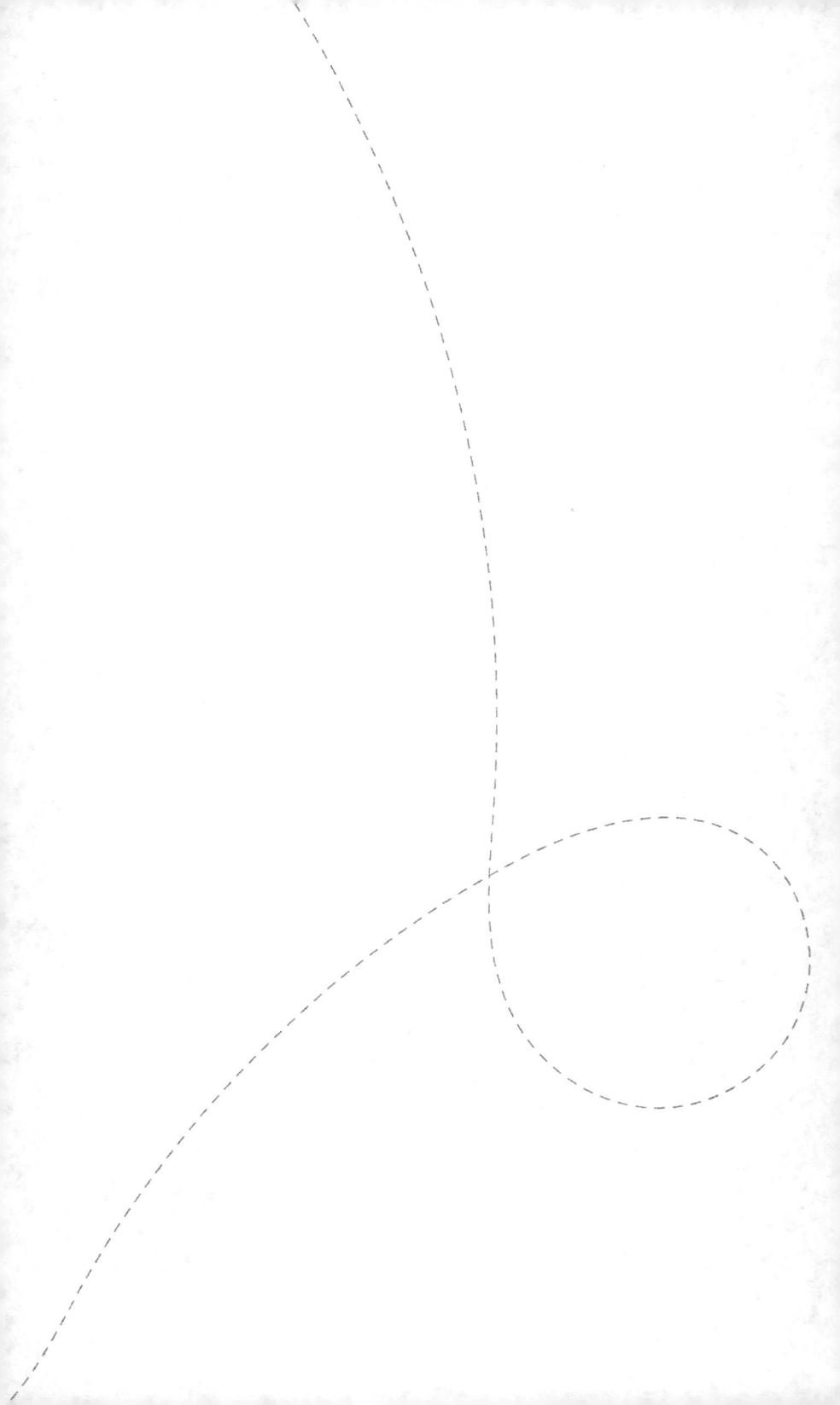

MY VULNERABILITY EXPERIMENT

Years ago, in my last corporate position, I engaged an executive coach. Over time and through our work together, I realized my deep interest in learning more about leadership coaching. At my coach's recommendation, I applied—and was thrilled to be accepted—to Georgetown University's prestigious Executive Certificate in Leadership Coaching program.

The program's curriculum requires four work days per month in person. Two weeks before I was to travel to Washington, DC, for the first time, my coach suggested using my Georgetown experience to practice vulnerability. The suggestion left me confused and uneasy, unsure exactly what he meant or why he suggested it. I even looked up the word *vulnerability* to be sure of its meaning: being open to emotional harm, taking risks, and showing one's true self. It still felt abstract, and I was unclear how it applied to me.

I asked my coach about it. To help clarify, he directed me to Brené Brown's TED Talks, particularly those linking vulnerability with shame. Brown's research has revealed how embracing vulnerability fosters deeper connection and authenticity. Watching her talks, something clicked, and I recognized that I, too, carried areas of shame in my life—two, specifically: my feelings about where I grew up and my sadness around being divorced.

As I reflected further, I realized I habitually avoided admitting I was from Bridgeport, Connecticut, preferring the safer "Fairfield County" instead. This shame traced back to a vivid teenage memory: While walking to the bathroom between classes, I overheard actor Paul Newman, who was visiting our high school as a potential movie filming location, describe Bridgeport as the "armpit of America" to our principal. For a reason I still don't necessarily understand, his words deeply wounded me, silently shaping my self-perception for years.

My divorce carried shame in a different way—not embarrassment, but sadness about feeling like a failure. This profound feeling led me to limit what I shared with others. To hold back.

So, at my coach's advice, I chose Georgetown as my experiment setting, a place where I would embrace vulnerability. On the train to DC, I gave myself permission to be fully authentic, open, and honest—regardless of others' judgments. On day one, I proudly introduced myself as being from Bridgeport for the first time in years. Joyfully, no judgment came. Instead, I felt immediate relief, freedom, and profound authenticity.

Later that afternoon, in a smaller group breakout session, I shared openly about my recent divorce, expressing genuine sadness and emotion. The group responded with incredible warmth and support, creating a safe space I hadn't experienced in years. One woman approached me afterward to say she was deeply touched by my honesty, revealing she was also navigating a divorce. Our heartfelt conversation fostered a meaningful connection and friendship that continues today.

My vulnerability experiment at Georgetown profoundly shifted my perspective. I learned firsthand that vulnerability isn't weakness; it's courage, connection, and authenticity. And I began to show up differently—not just personally but professionally. I became more open with my team, more willing to say "I don't know" or admit when something was hard. And something else shifted. When I dropped the shield, others did too. Meetings became more honest. Trust deepened. Relationships grew.

Today, whenever asked where I'm from, I confidently answer, "Bridgeport, Connecticut," often sharing my Paul Newman story with a smile. It no longer carries the same weight. It's just part of my story.

I highly recommend exploring vulnerability, perhaps starting with Brené Brown's insightful TED Talks, books, or podcasts. But even more, I invite you to try your own version of a vulnerability experiment. Pick one part of yourself you usually hold back. Then, in a safe space, practice being open. The outcome might surprise you—and unlock something more authentic in how you lead and connect.

JOURNALING EXERCISE

Practicing Vulnerability

1. **Present Reflection:** Think of a part of your personal or professional story that you tend to keep guarded.

   - What part of your experience do you often edit, soften, or hide?
   - What emotion—shame, fear, sadness, uncertainty—might be underneath that?
   - How might sharing even a small piece of this in a safe space create connection?

2. **Future Intention:** Choose one opportunity in the next week where you can practice vulnerability in a meaningful but manageable way.

   - What's one story, truth, or feeling you can share with more openness?
   - Who is a safe person (or where is a safe space) to try this?
   - What do you want to notice or learn from the experience? How can it help you professionally?

GENTLE REMINDER

Vulnerability isn't about oversharing—it's about showing up with honesty and heart. When you let go of the need to appear perfect, you give others permission to do the same.

Your truth is not too much. It's exactly what's needed to build trust, connection, and real leadership.

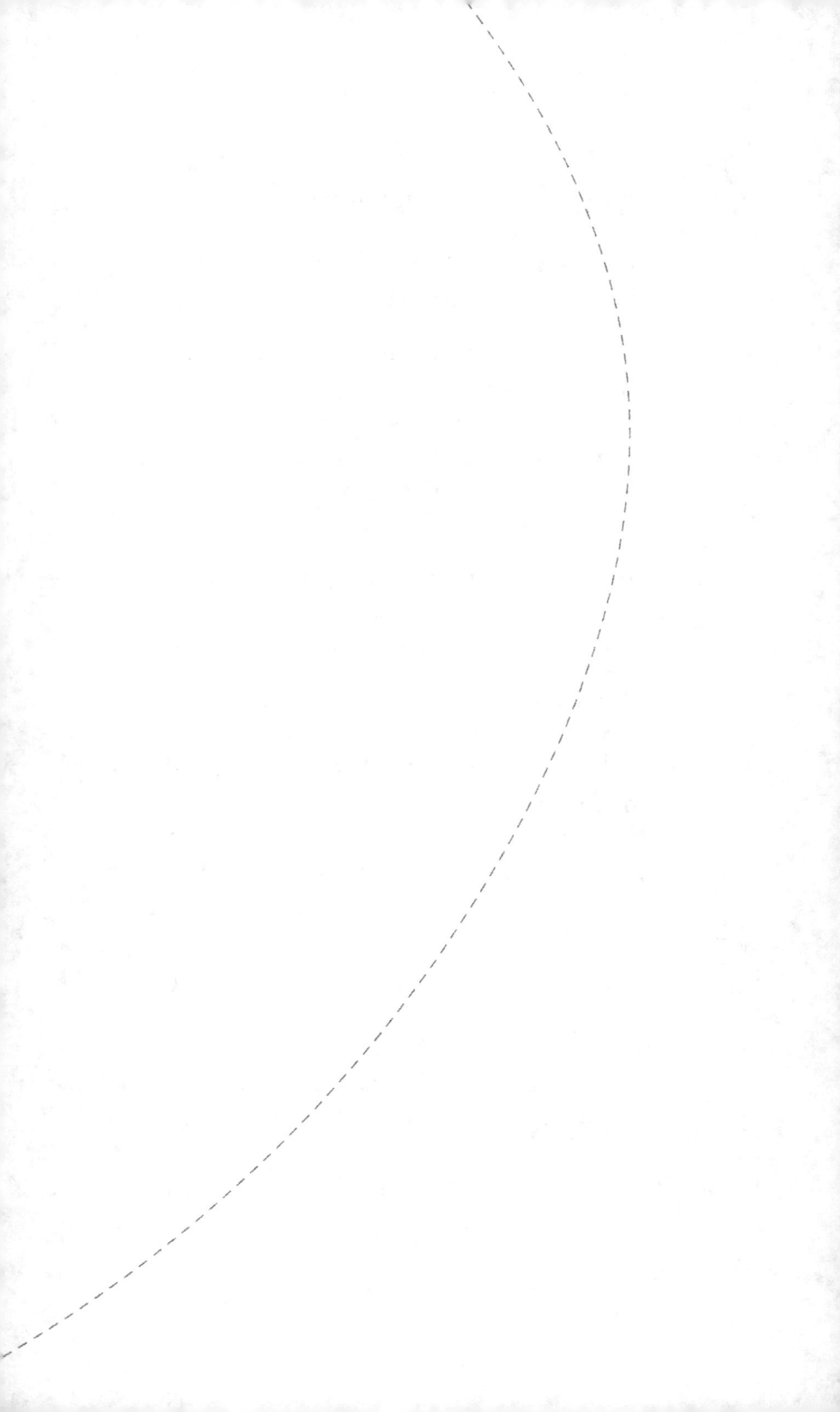

THE PEN IS IN YOUR HAND

HERE'S SOMETHING I'VE learned: The only thing people know about you is what you choose to tell them. If I told you I'm a leadership coach who's married with five children, you might believe me. But that's not true. (I *am* a leadership coach—but the rest? Not part of my story.)

This insight hit me years ago when a master-level coach said something I'll never forget: "You can write your story as the heroine in retreat . . . or the heroine in victory."

That was a moment that transformed how I saw myself—and how I began to tell my story. I realized I have the power to decide what narrative I want to live in. And I choose to be the heroine in victory. Not because everything in my life is perfect (far from it), but because I believe in possibility. I believe in hope. I believe in telling a story that lifts me up—and maybe inspires others, too.

When you begin to write your story from that place we've discussed throughout this book—one of strength, clarity, and purpose—it changes how you walk into a room. It becomes a way to affirm your values, your gifts, and your resilience. It helps you remember who you are, especially on the days when you forget.

Being the author of your story doesn't mean fabricating a version of yourself—it means choosing the lens through which you see your life. It means naming your strengths out loud. We now know it means vulnerability. And it means connecting the dots of your experiences and recognizing how much you've already overcome.

As I write this, I'm reminded of a conversation I had with one of my clients years ago. Colleen was a senior director at a large global technology company. She had significant responsibilities, leading critical corporate functions that were regularly discussed at the board level. She led a large team at work—and at home, she was married with four children under the age of six. When people heard that, she told me, they often asked her, "How do you do it?" Her answer was always, "I don't know."

When this came up in one of our coaching conversations, I realized Colleen was someone who had fallen into the habit of minimizing herself. Minimizing is when we downplay our abilities, deflect credit, or shrink our story to avoid seeming boastful. It's common—especially among high-performing women who've been conditioned to put others first.

We explored what might be causing her to respond that way. I held up the proverbial mirror, as coaches do, and asked her to answer the question again—but this time, truthfully and without apology. She paused and said, with quiet confidence: "I'm resourceful. I'm well-organized. I have a great husband and support system around me. I know my priorities, and I'm focused."

Her clarity was undeniable, and so was her strength. I encouraged her to make *that* her new answer—because it was true, and it honored the fullness of who she was. That moment was important for Colleen. She realized that she could be the author of her story—and tell it with confidence and pride.

The story you tell yourself—and others—matters. So, make it one worth rereading.

JOURNALING EXERCISE
Owning My Story

What story are you telling yourself—and is it the one you're truly living? The one you want to live?

1. **If someone asked you, "How do you do it all?" what would you typically say?**

2. **Now, ask yourself again—and this time, answer with honesty and pride.** What are the real strengths, supports, and choices that help you show up every day?

3. **Are there areas in which you tend to minimize yourself?** What would it look like to speak from a place of confidence instead?

4. **Imagine rewriting your story so that you are the *heroine/hero in victory*.** How would your next chapter begin?

GENTLE REMINDER

You are not defined by your past or boxed in by your present. You are the author, and the pen is in your hand. So, write a story that honors your truth—and lights the way forward.

WHAT PARENTING TAUGHT ME ABOUT LEADERSHIP

WHEN EMMA WAS two years old and navigating the "terrible twos" (although, let's be honest, her twos were never terrible), *time-out* was a popular parenting practice. Time-out is a discipline technique that involves placing your child in a very boring spot for a few minutes following unacceptable behavior, thereby removing them from the source of naughtiness. Many parents found it more effective than yelling or using other parenting techniques.

At the time, we were living in California in a long, one-level, ranch-style home—typical for the area. Emma's bedroom was at one end of our house, and the family room was at the other, with about a hundred feet in between. One day, while I was in the kitchen cooking dinner, I heard Emma, who was just learning to talk, coming down the hallway and grumbling, "Out, out, out." I stopped what I was doing and watched her hurry by, clutching her doll in both arms as she made her way toward the family room. There, in the corner, sat a small Winnie the Pooh chair. I watched as she tossed her lovely little doll into the chair while continuing to repeat, "Out, out, out." Emma was visibly upset and even shaking.

I was devastated. In that moment, I saw myself reflected back to me—in the very same way I had used time-out with Emma—and I was instantly grateful that I hadn't relied on this practice too often. Here was my precious little girl, teaching me a valuable lesson about patience and compassion. What I hadn't realized until that moment was that my intentional discipline technique had an unintentional consequence, one I didn't expect nor want. Time-out was upsetting to Emma, as likely was my behavior when I was placing her in it. I vowed then and there that I would never use time-out again. Later, I asked myself, "What sort of mother do I really want to be?" My answer was simple: I wanted to be a compassionate mother, someone my daughter could approach for anything, a mother who would teach calmly and explain, rather than be impatient or upset.

From that day forward, I kept my word. No more time-out. The lesson had been powerful. I'd realized that my daughter was watching my every move and emulating me more than I had known. It was so important for me to help her learn to show respect for others, maintain a positive outlook, uphold our family values, and manage anger effectively. Her role-playing had taught me the true meaning of *role modeling*. My behavior would help to shape how *she* would behave in relationships, in school, and throughout her life.

Since that day, I have done everything I can to be the best role model for my daughter. I often replay that "out, out, out" moment in my head, determined that she never again perceive me in that way. Of course, this doesn't mean I never lost my cool or yelled—after all, I am only human. But when I look back now, I can honestly say that I showed up as the mother I aspired to be, rather than who I was before.

Learning from our own behavior is part of being a good leader. I know that for me, paying attention to who I want to be—rather than just what I'm doing—has been an important lesson, one that I have implemented in many situations over the course of my leadership roles and human interactions.

How do you want to show up for those you love and serve?

JOURNALING EXERCISE

How Is My Leadership Impacting Others?

1. **Recall a moment when someone reflected your behavior back to you—either literally or figuratively.**

   • How did that moment make you feel?
   • What did it teach you about the influence you have?

2. **Pause to consider who is quietly watching how you move through the world right now.**

   • A child? A teammate? A mentee?
   • What might you be teaching them—intentionally or unintentionally?

3. **Think of a behavior or habit that someone close to you has picked up from you.**

   • Is it something you're proud of—or something you'd rather change?

4. **Imagine that your daily actions were being recorded and replayed for someone you deeply care about.**

   • What parts would you want them to model?
   • What parts would you feel compelled to explain?

5. **What's one small change you can make in how you respond, lead, or care for others that could positively shape someone else's path?**

GENTLE REMINDER

You are always leading, whether you mean to or not. In quiet moments and heated ones, others are watching—not for perfection, but for guidance. Lead with the grace you'd want mirrored back to you.

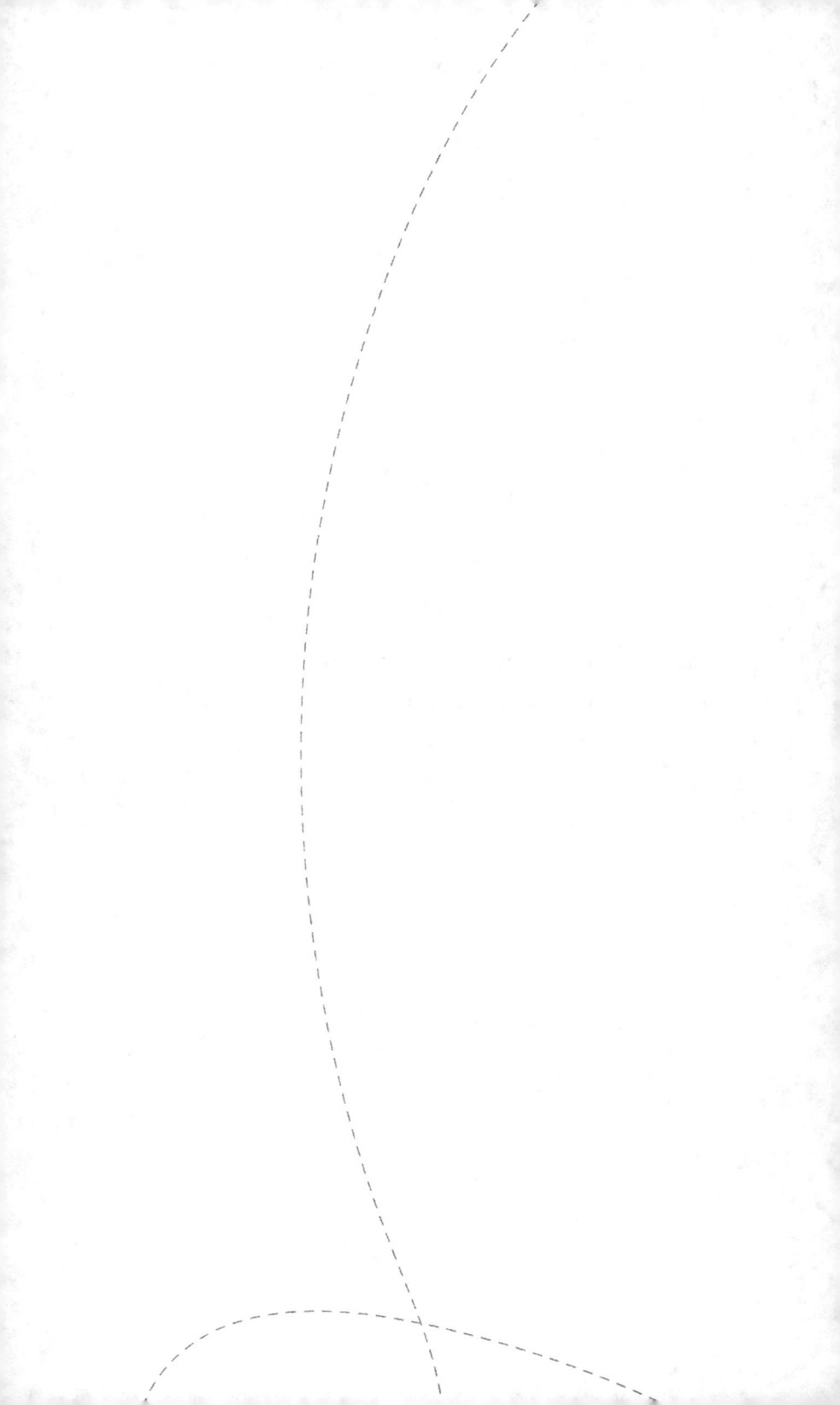

LEADERSHIP HAPPENS THROUGH LANGUAGE

ONE OF MY favorite conversations to have with clients begins with a simple question: *"How does leadership occur?"*

Often, they look puzzled at first, expecting this to be a trick question. Their answers then vary—usually pointing to behaviors that motivate others toward results. But when asked for my perspective, I share this: *Leadership occurs through language.*

Others have different definitions, of course. One that stands out to me arose from a memorable encounter at work. I mentioned earlier how fortunate I was to work in Sun's Leadership Development Group for a few years. One of my most exciting assignments was to help produce the biannual Sun Leadership Conference, where our CEO, Scott McNealy, brings together the top two hundred leaders at Sun for a two-day event. One full day was always devoted entirely to leadership-skill building and the other to motivational speeches and company strategy. We typically invited an inspirational external speaker; on one occasion, it was General Colin Powell, former Chairman of the Joint Chiefs of Staff.

I was honored to brief his office ahead of his visit to our Santa Clara campus, and on the day of the event, I was asked to personally greet him when he arrived by limousine. It was thrilling to meet him in person and settle him into our "green room" offstage, where he could prepare for his lecture.

During our quiet moment together, I asked him a question I couldn't resist: *"How do you define leadership?"* His response was immediate: *"Follow me."* Then he added, "If you look behind you and there is no one following, then you are not a leader."

I loved the simplicity and clarity of his answer. It has stayed with me ever since.

I often share this story with my clients and pair it with my belief that leadership lives in the words we speak. To illustrate this, I sometimes invite my client into a brief scenario: *Let's imagine we're in a high-stakes moment—things are moving fast, and quick decisions matter. I'm the leader, and I say to you, "Take that hill."* That moment of direction, of clarity, of language that moves others to act—that's leadership.

We then explore together something called *"leadership speech acts"*—verbal expressions that generate action. In everyday business life, these often show up as *requests* and *offers*. At its core, a request or offer is language that creates a future that otherwise would not exist. When those requests or offers are accepted, they become *commitments*—and commitments are the building blocks of leadership and trust.

Many of my clients enter coaching conversations overwhelmed by the workload they've taken on. One of my early observations is that they say "yes" too quickly—when they really need to say "no," propose a counteroffer, or pause before committing.

I learned this the hard way myself. Early in my career, I said yes to leading a high-profile project while already juggling too many responsibilities. I wanted to be seen as capable and helpful—but I ended up delivering it late, under enormous stress, and not at the quality I expected of myself. That experience taught me that saying yes without boundaries isn't generosity—it's self-betrayal.

When I coach, I teach that there are four legitimate responses to any request:

1. **Yes**
2. **No**
3. **Counteroffer**
4. **Commit-to-commit** (As in, "Let me get back to you by Friday.")

Most of my clients struggle with saying no out of fear—fear of disappointing others, seeming unhelpful, or losing future opportunities. But here's the truth: *Time is not scalable.* You can't buy more of it. After all, as a leader your reputation depends not just on saying yes—but on *delivering* on what you say yes to.

From personal experience, I've found that most requests are more flexible than we assume. Timing, scope, and deliverables can often be negotiated—but only if we pause long enough to ask. When I'm coaching clients on executive presence, influence, or time management, we often return to this foundation: *Speak. Choose. Protect.* Speak with clarity. Choose your commitments wisely. Protect your energy, your time, and your word.

I still think about General Powell's words: *"Follow me."* Leadership isn't control or charisma—it's language that earns trust and inspires action. It's about communicating in a way that invites others to step forward with you.

JOURNALING EXERCISE
The Power of Leadership Language

Leadership happens through language—the words you choose, the commitments you make, and the boundaries you set. **For this exercise, write about:**

1. **Language and Action:** Think of a recent time when you made a request, offer, or agreement. How did your words help shape the future or influence others' actions?

2. **Saying Yes and No:**

   - How often do I say yes automatically—without fully considering my time, energy, or priorities?
   - What would change if I paused before answering— and was therefore able to choose yes, no, counter-offer, or commit-to-commit more intentionally?

3. **Managing My Commitments:**

   - What commitments have I made recently that feel aligned, energizing, and doable?
   - Are there any commitments I wish I had declined or negotiated differently?

4. **Strengthening Leadership Presence:**

   - What is one small change I can make in my communication—starting today—to lead with more clarity, courage, and integrity?

GENTLE REMINDER

Every time you speak, you have the power to shape a future that didn't exist before. Lead thoughtfully. Speak intentionally. Protect your time, your energy, and your word.

PART V
The Growth Edge

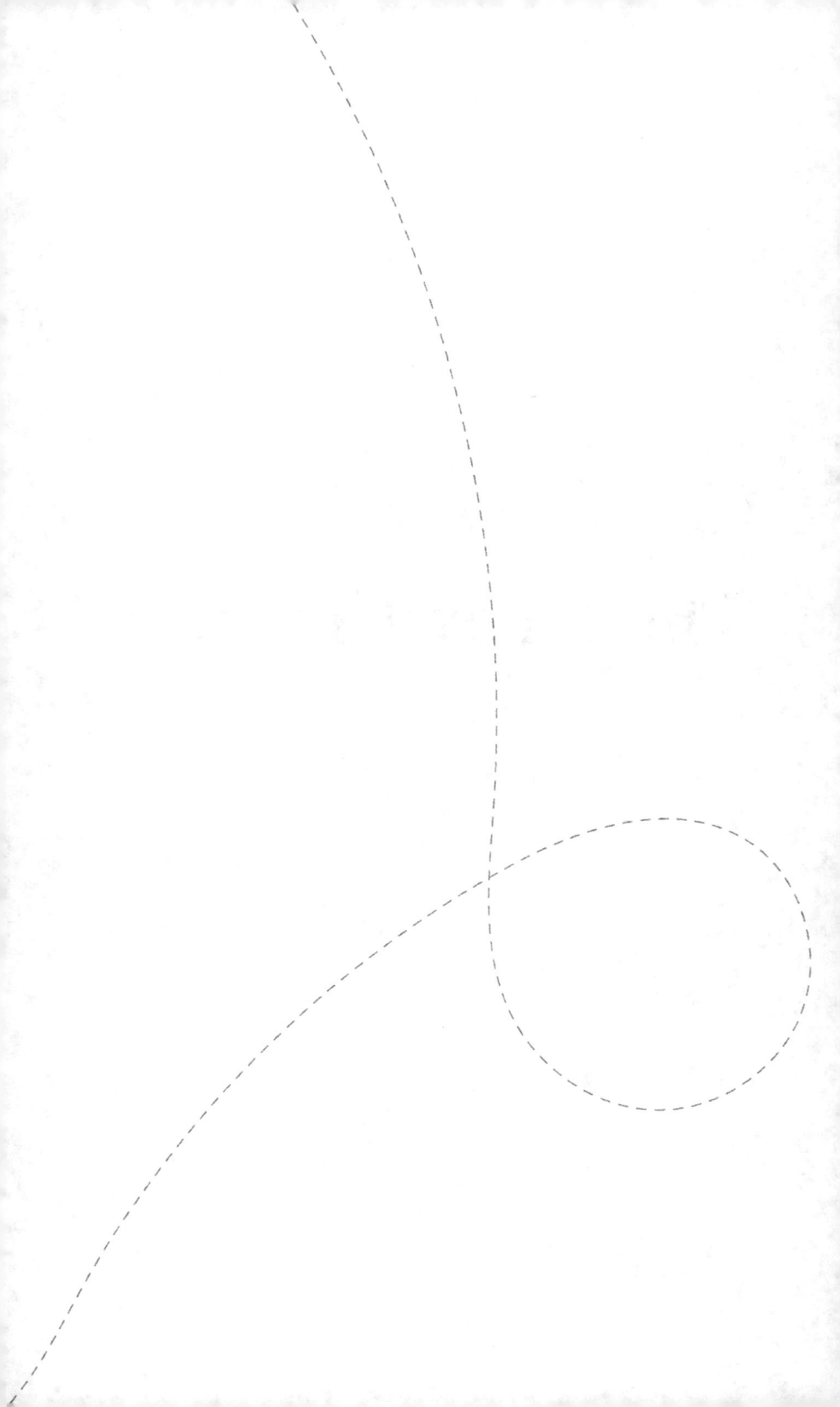

DON'T OVERVALUE EXPERTISE

WHEN I BECAME a leadership coach, Georgetown encouraged me to pick a niche for my practice. Even before beginning my formal coaching education, I knew I wanted to focus on coaching women and men in technology organizations. After more than twenty years of experience working in tech companies and promotions into executive director roles, I knew this was where I could have the greatest impact on future generations.

A bit here about my history. Interestingly, despite what I would define as a successful career, I never studied computer science, technology, or programming. Actually, I had very little technical computer expertise. What propelled me to the positions I held at Sun Microsystems and Merck was not technical mastery—it was leadership presence and thought leadership in areas like process improvement and organizational change management. These became my career-defining skills, and I developed high levels of competency (and therefore confidence) in both.

When I first joined Merck, I entered through the Merck Sigma organization. After Merck's merger with Schering-Plough, that Six Sigma function was disbanded. I moved into the IT organization to work closely with the CIO and his leadership team, helping drive the CIO's transformation agenda. I loved the work – it was perfectly aligned with my value-based career compass (as discussed in Story 12).

Over time, the CIO's trust in me grew. Several years later, on a Thursday afternoon, he approached me in the hallway and told me that, starting Monday, he planned to move the PMO organization—a large team of about two hundred people—under my leadership. Without hesitation, I replied, "Yes, I'll do whatever you need me to do."

I had no idea what I was signing up for. At that moment, I wasn't even sure what "PMO" stood for. I knew the "MO" meant Management Office, but I wasn't clear whether the "P" referred to Project, Program, Product, or Portfolio. That evening, after dinner, I googled the term. I learned that it stood for Project Management Office—and it carried implications for the other Ps as well. The more I read about PMOs, the more anxious I became. Leading a PMO certainly had never been on my list of career aspirations, and now I was about to step into that very role.

What I drew upon in that moment was everything I had learned up until then—particularly from my leadership experiences at Sun Microsystems. I instinctively knew that I didn't need to become a PMO *expert*. With over two hundred people in the organization, my job wasn't to master project management; it was to build and empower a high-performing leadership team, create clarity, communicate with confidence, and support my leaders to be the best versions of themselves.

That's exactly what I did. I hired what I call the BOBs—the Best of the Best—and trusted them to lead their areas of expertise. My role was to stay informed, support them, and most importantly, stay out of their way when necessary. I showed up with leadership presence and did my best to empower them to thrive.

I love sharing this personal story with my technology clients—many of whom believe they need one more skill, one more certification, to advance their careers. I never intend to diminish the value of technical training or expertise. However, in my experience, a strong focus on leadership skills and presence can often have a greater payoff than simply accumulating more technical certifications.

As you think about your own future and career advancement, I invite you to reflect: Are you overvaluing expertise? What if, instead, you focused on showing up with greater leadership presence, able to influence senior leaders, align stakeholders across major initiatives, and lead with confidence?

From my experience—both as an executive and as a coach—focusing on leadership is the true accelerator.

This is why, many years later, I ultimately made the bold decision to leave a company, a job, a team, and a salary I loved—to devote the rest of my career to leadership coaching. It was my way of aligning my sense of purpose with my work. My hope is to make an impact on the next generation of leaders—helping them realize that leadership is the answer.

Balancing Expertise and Presence

Your technical skills may have opened the door, but your leadership presence will carry you through the next stages of your career. Today, explore how you can build your leadership identity beyond just expertise. **Consider your current leadership presence and address the following questions:**

1. **My Current Mindset:** How much of my confidence today comes from being an "expert" in a certain skill, role, or technical area?

2. **Expanding My Value:** Beyond technical skills, what leadership qualities do I already bring to the table? (Examples: inspiring others, communicating vision, building relationships, influencing outcomes)

3. **Focusing on Leadership:** If I shifted even 10 to 20 percent of my development energy away from technical expertise and toward strengthening leadership presence, what new possibilities might open for me?

4. **The Next Brave Step:** What is one leadership behavior—such as influence, communication, strategic thinking, or presence—that I can focus on strengthening in the next three months?

GENTLE REMINDER

*The next level of your career isn't about knowing more—
it's about becoming more. More courageous, more visible, and
more trusted to lead others forward.*

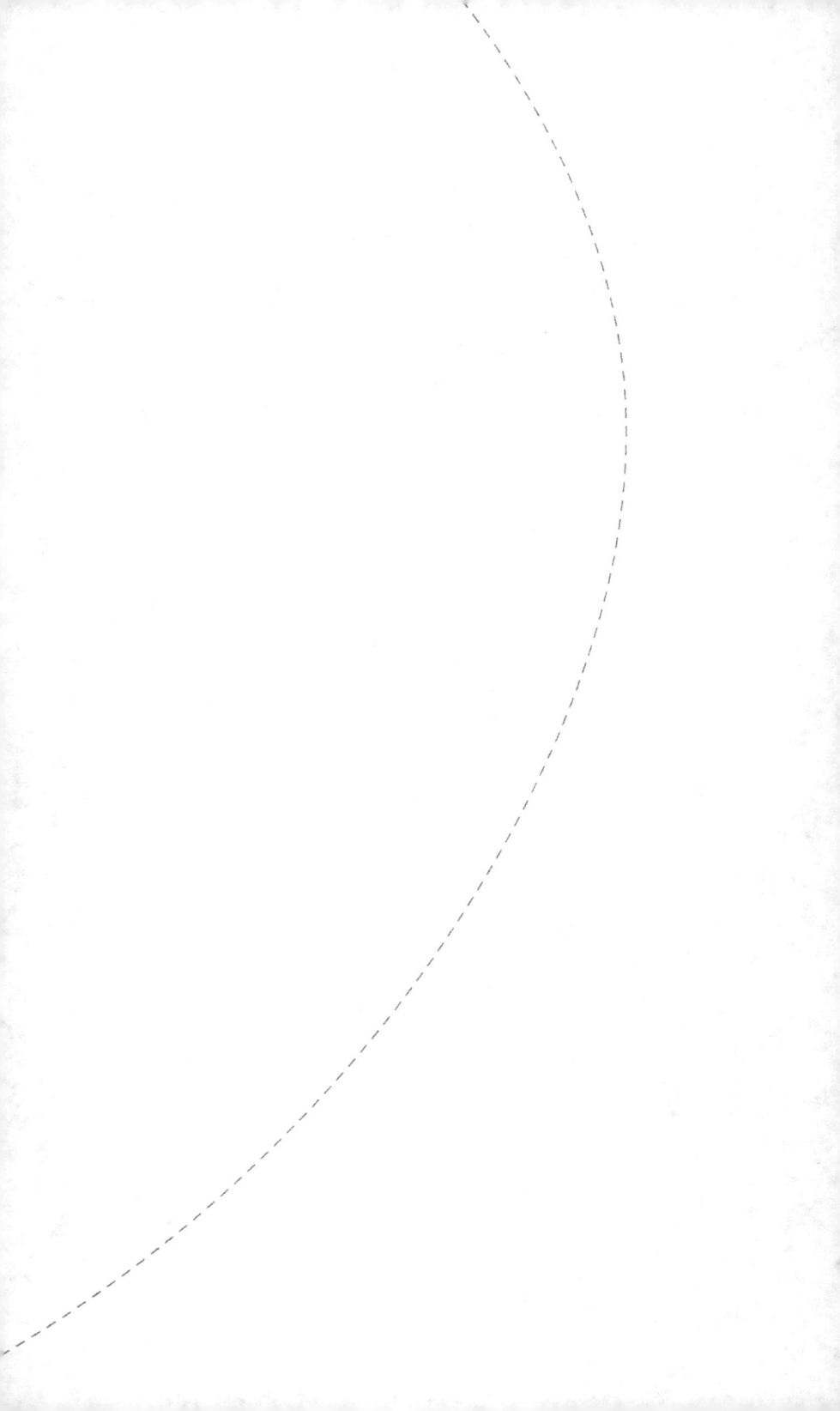

MEASURE IN BABY STEPS

The Hidden Progress of Strategic Leadership

MANY OF MY clients come into coaching with the goal of improving their strategic thinking and decision-making skills. These are individuals who are highly competent—often with deep technical expertise developed through years of managing day-to-day IT responsibilities like troubleshooting, implementing upgrades, and leading large projects. But when it comes to seeing the big picture—connecting their work to long-term goals, aligning with the organization's mission, or influencing enterprise direction—they often feel stuck.

Why? Because they've been rewarded for execution, not for seeing the holistic and strategic picture.

A common habit I see in these clients is their inability to say "no." They're conditioned to respond to every urgent request, to solve immediate problems, to *do* rather than *pause*.

As we discussed a few stories ago, this reactive, pause-less pattern keeps them in the weeds. And as one rises through the ranks—especially into director-level and above—the ability to think and operate strategically becomes not just valuable but essential.

As leaders grow, their role shifts from doing the work themselves to discerning what matters most, setting direction, and creating space for others to thrive.

One metaphor I love to use when coaching on this topic is "seeing the forest for the trees." It means being able to step back from the details (the trees) and recognize the bigger picture (the forest). Sometimes people get so caught up in small tasks, problems, or details that they lose sight of the overall purpose, strategy, or goal. This phrase is a reminder to zoom out and understand how all the pieces fit together.

A few years ago, while visiting Olympic National Forest in Washington State, I had a striking realization. As I drove through the forest, I could only see a few trees at a time. When I stopped to explore a single massive tree, I got lost in its thick bark, sprawling limbs, and detailed textures. It was beautiful, yes—and I'm glad I witnessed its beauty. Yet I also realized that in focusing so closely on one tree, I temporarily lost all sight of the vast, stunning expanse of the forest and the magnificent ecosystem surrounding me, including the rocky coastlines and the glacier-covered mountains.

It's the same in corporate life. Unless you are sitting in the strategy office, it's easy to become absorbed in the work directly in front of you—your team, your tasks, your deadlines. The immediate details cause you to lose sight of the broader organizational ecosystem: the customers you serve, the strategic priorities you support, and the long-term outcomes you're meant to enable.

Throughout my career in high-tech, I often found myself in meetings where we jumped right into reviewing action items. Occasionally, I would interrupt to ask simple questions: "Can we just take a moment to revisit why we're here? What problem are we solving? Who are we solving it for?" These small pauses often led to big realignments. When teams reconnected to purpose, to the bigger picture, energy shifted. Decisions got smarter. Noise gave way to clarity.

Early in my career at Merck, I had the opportunity to get certified in a strategy execution framework taught by Daryl Conner. It introduced a simple yet powerful Venn diagram of three interlocking circles: Intent, People, and Delivery.

- *Intent* is about clarity—What are we trying to achieve, why does it matter, and who are we serving?
- *People* focuses on engagement—How do we ensure we have the right sponsorship? How do we keep stakeholders informed, aligned, and contributing?

- *Delivery* is the execution muscle—Making it happen with discipline and accountability.

In IT, 80 to 90 percent of energy goes to delivery and execution. Research confirms this imbalance—most managers are stuck in urgent tasks, with little space for strategy. That gap creates real strategic risk. The fix begins when leaders shift some of their focus from doing to discerning—clarifying purpose, engaging stakeholders, and making space for reflection.

As a corporate leader at Sun Microsystems, another tool that helped me manage strategic risk when leading cross-functional initiatives came from my time becoming certified as a Six Sigma Black Belt. One of the most powerful tools I learned was the XY Flow Down. At its core, it's a method for mapping how the *outcome* you're trying to achieve (the Y) is driven by specific contributing factors (the X's). In short: Y is a function of X.

This tool helped Sun teams get clear on their true outcome—what success really looked like—and assess whether the things they were working on were actually contributing to it. May seem like a basic concept, but it was, in fact, eye-opening. A colleague and I even coined a phrase that still rings true today: "Most teams are confusing activity with achievement." They're obsessing over the *little x's* without asking whether those are truly advancing the *BIG Y*.

Strategic leadership demands that shift in focus. It's not about doing more; it's about doing what matters.

And when you begin to work more strategically, something else happens—you find you need to change your measurement system. When I was at Sun and leading large-scale, cross-functional strategic initiatives, I remember one particularly challenging period when it felt like we were spinning our wheels. I vented to my coach, telling him I thought we were failing and certainly not making enough progress. He stopped me in my tracks.

"Anne," he said, "you know what your problem is? You're using the wrong ruler. You're measuring success in yards when you should be measuring it in baby steps. You're leading the team beautifully. You're moving in the right direction. But because the wins are incremental, you don't see them."

Strategic work often unfolds slowly. The shifts are nuanced. But when you look back and trace the baby steps—each conversation, alignment, insight, decision, small success—you begin to see just how far you've come.

At Merck, I learned to become an "Intent Manager." Instead of jumping into the *how*, I started with the *why*. I asked better questions. I aligned stakeholders before assigning tasks. I recognized that strategy is almost never about speed; it's about direction, clarity, and disciplined focus. Strategic leaders don't just get things done. They get the *right things* done. And in a world that rewards busy-ness, it takes real courage to pause and climb above the trees—to see the forest, reconnect to intent, and lead from there.

Baby Steps Toward Strategic Leadership

Present Reflection:

- Where in your current role are you still measuring success in "yards" instead of "baby steps"?
- Think about the past week: Where have you been focused on activity over making true progress?
- What habits or patterns keep you in execution mode, reacting rather than reflecting?

Future Intention:

- Looking ahead, how can you create space to pause before diving into action? Be as specific as you can.
- What's one strategic question you could begin asking—of yourself or your team—to stay connected to the bigger picture?
- How might shifting your focus from doing to discerning change the way you lead?

GENTLE REMINDER

Strategic leadership isn't about doing more, it's about asking the right questions, aligning others around a shared purpose, and making deliberate choices that move you forward, even if only by baby steps.

The most impactful leaders aren't always the busiest— they're the clearest.

THE SANDBOX MINDSET

Practice, Presence, Progress

IN MY COACHING work, I love using analogies to help clients see themselves and their challenges more clearly. One of my favorites is this: *Leadership is like a sandbox.*

When I was a child, I had a sandbox in the backyard. I adored it. I spent hours shoveling wet sand into different molds—castles, conch shells, starfish—and gently turning them over to reveal what I had made. Sometimes the shape would hold perfectly. Other times, it would crumble into a pile of soggy nothing. And when it did, I never cried or gave up. I simply brushed the mess away with a flick of my wrist and started again. I loved the feeling of creative freedom, of trying again, of *practicing* until something beautiful emerged.

Great leadership works the same way. Leadership is not about getting it right the first time. It's about showing up every day with intention and a willingness to experiment. It's about paying attention to what works, letting go of what doesn't, and having the courage to try again—with humility and heart. It's about practice.

Of course, there have been plenty of times in my own career when my leadership castle completely crumbled. I can still remember the feeling—those days when I felt like my leadership had gone right out the window. What triggered those moments was almost always one of two things: working with someone whose values were totally different from mine, or trying to navigate murky organizational politics.

While at Sun Microsystems, I worked alongside a colleague who was highly action-oriented, non-compassionate, passive aggressive, and, at times, even vindictive. This colleague was reactionary as well. I, however, was more strategic—I liked to pause, think, and act only when I believed it would create value. I felt value in the pause. Needless to say, we didn't see eye to eye. She began telling coworkers that I was ineffective, and I began complaining to my boss about her.

One day, during a conversation with my boss, he looked at me and asked the $64,000 coaching question: *"What is it about you that can't work with her?"* It was a simple question, but with profound implications for me.

In that moment, I realized it wasn't about her at all—it was about *me*. If I wanted to lead effectively in that environment, I needed to shift my own behavior. So, I sat down and made a list of all the things about her that triggered me. I kept that list in front of me and treated every day like an experiment in the sandbox.

I tried different approaches. I adjusted my mindset. I chose curiosity over criticism. Over time, we not only learned to work together—we became friends.

That's the beauty of the sandbox. It gives you permission to try. And to try again.

One of my male clients embraced this metaphor completely. He's a master facilitator and finds himself in meetings with a wide variety of participants—some friendly, some quiet, some difficult. His aspiration is to be a truly remarkable leader: approachable, balanced, present, supportive, inspiring, and growth-minded. He now sees every meeting as part of his sandbox. Every conversation is a new mold to fill, a new opportunity to practice his leadership with intention. And yes, to leave room for mistakes.

He recently had a meeting with a notoriously difficult senior executive in his division. In the past, their conversations were strained and unproductive. But this time, he approached the situation differently—he grounded himself beforehand, got clear on his intent, and chose to show up fully present and open. The result? A productive, respectful dialogue. Nothing about the executive had changed—but everything about *my client's* leadership had.

So, if you want to build your own leadership sandbox, you don't need wood or sand. You need something even more powerful: a clear mindset. Start by putting words to what "good" leadership looks like for you. Write it down. Then, each day, step into your sandbox and bring it to life— one conversation, one decision, one experiment at a time. And when something crumbles? Brush it away, learn what you can, and try again tomorrow.

JOURNALING EXERCISE

Practicing Leadership in the Sandbox

Present Reflection:

- Think back to a recent moment where your leadership didn't go quite the way you intended. What happened? What "crumbled" in the conversation, meeting, or dynamic?
- Rather than judging yourself, pause to consider: What external triggers or internal patterns might have influenced your reaction?
- How did you respond—and what did you learn about yourself in the process?

Future Intention:

- Now imagine stepping into your leadership "sandbox" tomorrow with fresh eyes and an open heart.
- What's one relationship, conversation, or challenge where you'd like to experiment with a new approach?
- What mindset or intention could you bring to help you lead with more presence, curiosity, or confidence in that moment?

GENTLE REMINDER

You don't have to be perfect to be influential. Leadership isn't about flawless execution—it's about showing up, trying new moves, and learning as you go. Every day in the sandbox is another chance to shape the leader you are becoming.

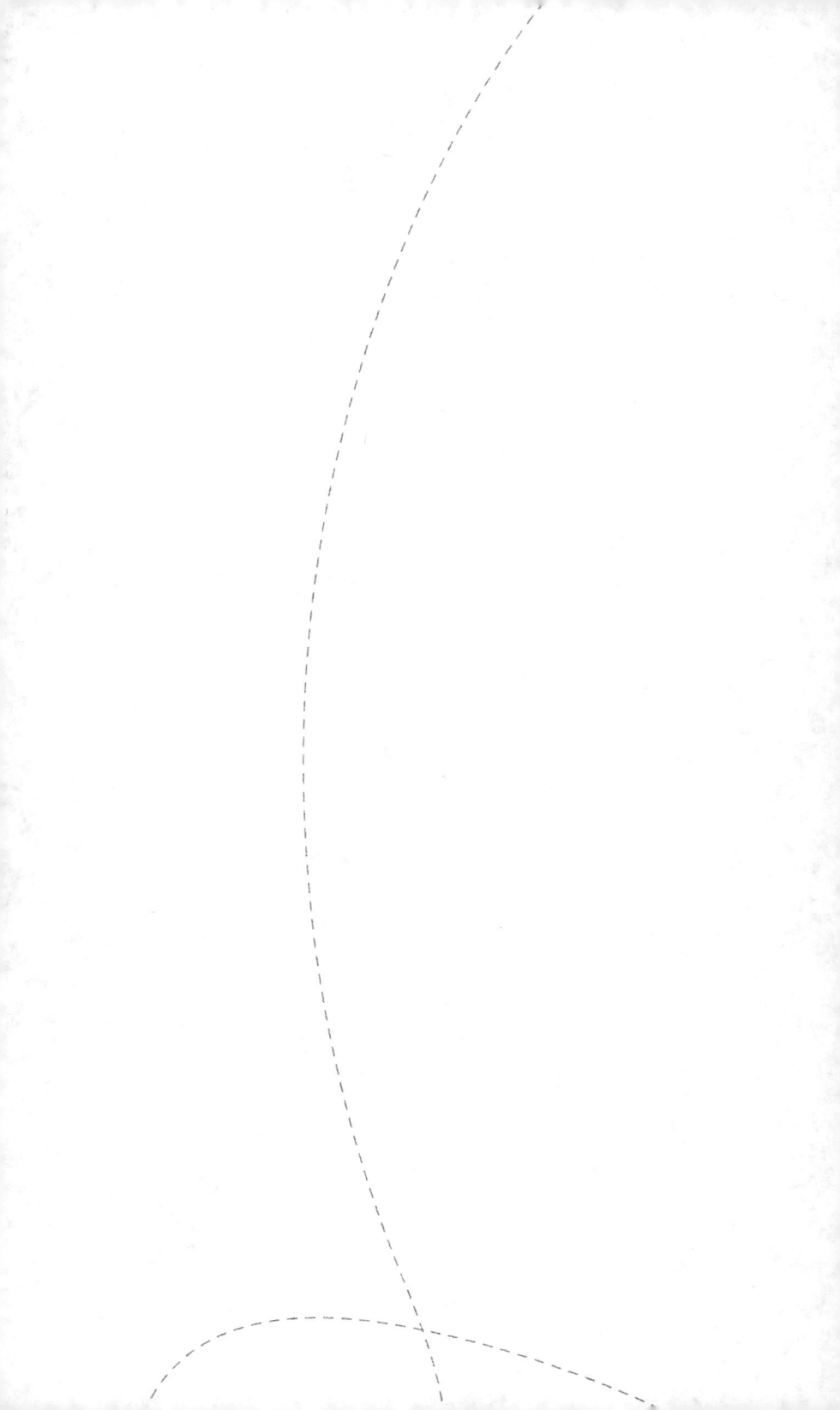

SOFT SKILLS AREN'T SOFT— THEY'RE ESSENTIAL

ONE OF THE most difficult experiences of my career came during a major transition. When I joined Merck and relocated my family from California to New Jersey, it was a huge life change. I carried around a lot of guilt—especially for taking my daughter, Emma, out of a school she loved in the middle of sixth grade. I kept reassuring myself that the opportunity would be worth it. But what I walked into caught me off guard.

My new boss had a military background and led with a command-and-control style that was very different from anything I was used to. He was technically strong and highly structured—but emotionally closed off. Rather than invite collaboration, he barked orders. And he struggled to connect with people. He never asked me about my family nor seemed to care about how we were managing the cross-country relocation.

On my very first day, he wasn't there to greet me—he was traveling. I found a typed list on my desk with several assignments and the names of key colleagues to meet. I got to work, eager to learn and make an impact. When he returned, we met briefly. He shared a high-level overview of my deliverables, then ended the meeting early. I was still new to the company, new to the industry, and I didn't have enough context to move forward confidently. I left feeling overwhelmed.

The next day, I peeked into his office and asked him gently if he would be willing to meet again for clarification. He agreed, although I heard reluctance in his voice. I came prepared with questions, ready to better understand the work ahead. But the more I asked, the more visibly irritated he became. I calmly explained that I wasn't challenging him—I just wanted to understand the full picture. That's when he raised his voice and said, *"Do I need to reprimand you?!"* I was stunned. I had never been spoken to like that in my entire life or career.

I walked out of his office and sat at my desk questioning everything. Had I made the right decision? I had moved three thousand miles for this. I had so much at stake—not just professionally but personally. And the person tasked with leading me lacked the one thing that mattered most to me in my professional relationships: emotional intelligence—the ability to relate.

Months later, I learned I wasn't the only one who had struggled. Several colleagues had voiced concerns to management about his leadership style—especially his inability to build trust or communicate effectively. Eventually, those patterns caught up with him. He was involuntarily separated from the company.

Now that I'm a leadership coach, I can look back at that experience differently. At the time, I internalized much of the stress and second-guessed my own instincts. But today, I coach leaders through similar dynamics—helping them understand that technical competence alone doesn't make someone effective. The ability to build trust, foster psychological safety, and communicate with empathy is what distinguishes a manager from a *true leader*.

Today, technical skills like cloud computing, AI, UX design, and app development may get you the interview—but soft skills are what secure the job, earn trust, and define long-term success. In my life, I've yet to read or write a job description that doesn't include soft skills. Collaboration, confidence, conflict management, adaptability, and the ability to handle ambiguity are all essential—not optional.

In a recent *Forbes* article, Jeff Weiner, former CEO of LinkedIn, said it plainly: "A big misconception about managing compassionately is that it's a "soft" skill. Most compassionate people I know are typically the strongest. "

When Google studied its most effective employees, STEM expertise came in last. What rose to the top? Communication. Active listening. Empathy. Problem solving.

And yet, soft skills are often the hardest to develop. Most leaders I coach don't lack intelligence or skillsets—they lack awareness. They haven't had the space or support to reflect on how they show up, how they're perceived, or how they impact those around them. They've sharpened technical skills while letting their relational muscles atrophy.

Many organizations are trying to bridge the gap through coaching, training programs, and tools like the Leadership Architect Suite—originally developed by Lominger International (now part of Korn Ferry). It's a practical, research-based toolkit that helps identify and develop the competencies leaders need to succeed—whether you're hiring, promoting, or coaching for growth. But in my experience, true leadership growth doesn't come from checking a box—it comes from practice, feedback, and the willingness to grow from hard moments.

So, here's the truth. If you want to lead people—not just manage tasks—you must develop your relational skills. Not because they're soft but because they're *everything*.

JOURNALING EXERCISE
Emphasizing My Soft Skills

Remember, leadership isn't about titles—it's about how you show up with and for others. Take time to reflect on your "soft skills" today and consider where you want to grow.

1. **My Current Strengths:** Which leadership "soft skills" (communication, empathy, adaptability, confidence, conflict management, etc.) come naturally to me?

2. **Areas for Growth:** Which leadership skill(s) could I develop more intentionally? *(Think about moments in which challenges have arisen—difficult conversations, team dynamics, navigating uncertainty, and others.)*

3. **Commitment to Growth:**

    - Choose *one* leadership skill you want to strengthen over the next three months.
    - Write a simple action plan. Then ask yourself: How will I practice it? Where will I apply it? How will I know I'm making progress?

GENTLE REMINDER

Soft skills aren't soft. They're the bedrock of meaningful leadership. The way you make people feel—the space you create, the tone you set, the trust you build—that is what they'll remember. That is what creates impact.

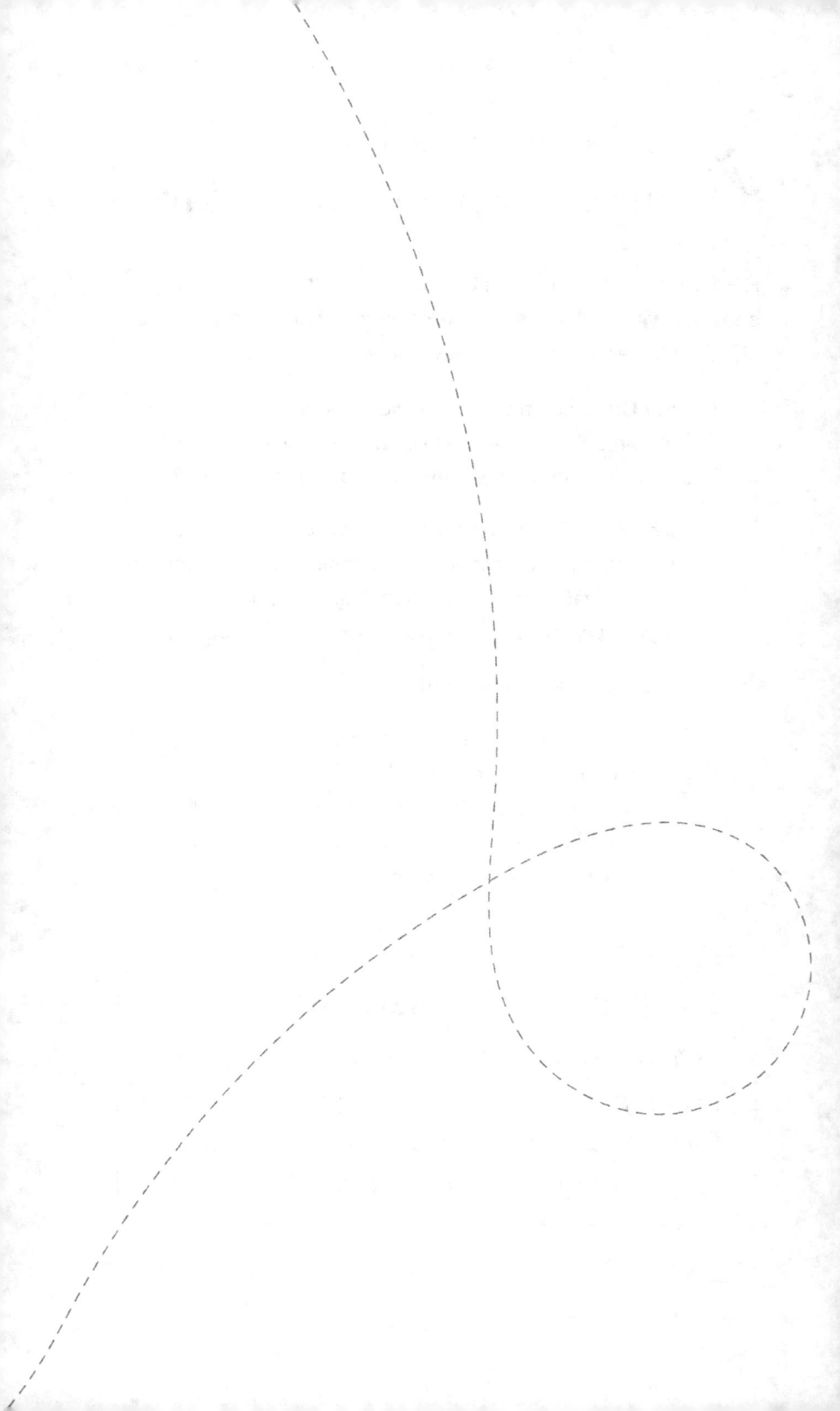

THE PERFECTION PARADOX

Badge or Burden?

MANY OF MY clients—especially women—struggle with perfectionism. They're bright, accomplished, and driven, yet carry an invisible burden: the desire to be flawless in every area of their lives. They want the perfect home, the perfect partner, the perfect wedding, the perfect work product, the perfect body, the perfect children—all while being the perfect mother, wife, and employee. It's exhausting just to type it.

What I've learned over the years is how deeply this mindset actually holds them back. Perfection becomes a standard, a pursuit, and—at first—a badge of honor. But over time, that badge starts to feel more like a burden. These women set impossibly high expectations for themselves. They're terrified of making mistakes, which leads to over-planning, over-working, and over-thinking. They're their own harshest critics.

Even when these women outperform their peers, they rarely feel satisfied. The bar keeps rising. They're never done. Then they find themselves in a vicious cycle: effort without ease, achievement without joy. Mistakes—natural, necessary parts of learning—feel like failures. And when things inevitably fall short of perfect for them, they spiral into disappointment and self-doubt. Ironically, the thing they're chasing—perfection—is often what stands in the way of their happiness.

One woman I coached years ago embodied these traits. Sarah was talented and driven but completely overwhelmed. She was the stereotype of "perfectly put together." When I asked what was going on, she described a project that had consumed her for over two weeks. Still, she wasn't ready to send it to her boss—she planned to work on it for several more days.

Knowing her perfectionist tendencies, I gently asked, "On a scale from zero to one hundred, how complete is your draft right now?" She replied, "About eighty." I offered her a challenge: "Would you be willing to send it as is and just see what happens?"

After some hesitation, Sarah agreed. The following week, she came back smiling. "My boss said it was perfect," she told me. "He loved it." We talked about what she learned: that all those extra hours she planned to spend tweaking weren't necessary. She not only delivered ahead of schedule but also saved herself stress, had many more hours back in her life, and felt proud and relieved.

As I work with these high-potential, hyper-driven women, I feel enormous empathy. Many trace their perfectionism back to childhood—with its parental pressure, high expectations, and repeated messages like *be a good girl, get straight A's, don't ask for help,* and *you can do it all.* Out of their mouths, I hear the voice of their younger selves—still trying to earn approval, still afraid of being "not enough."

They wear the perfectionist badge with pride, not realizing the weight it's putting on their shoulders. I hear stories of procrastination, paralysis, and burnout. For these clients, delegation becomes nearly impossible—"No one can do it as well as I can." And still, they don't feel good enough. Or even, *enough.*

When I gently suggest, "There's no such thing as perfect," they often look puzzled—like I've just told them the sky is green. That's when I share two quotes that have always helped me:

> There is nothing known as "perfect." It's only those imperfections which we choose not to see.
> —Albert Einstein

> Perfection is not attainable. But if we chase perfection, we can catch excellence.
> —Vince Lombardi

I ask them to pause and reflect:

- What if that badge you've been wearing is actually a burden?
- What if chasing perfection is keeping you from experiencing fulfillment, freedom, and joy?

And then something shifts. I listen carefully as they consider the new insights that begin to emerge:

- Maybe perfectionism has held me back.
- Maybe I've been wasting time trying to polish what was already shiny enough.
- Maybe excellence—not perfection—is the real goal.

Sometimes, embracing what's known as the "80/20 rule" can feel like a lifeline. Think of the 80/20 rule as a reminder that most of your impact usually comes from a small portion of your effort—so the key is to know which twenty percent really matters. Letting go of the impossibility of "perfect" doesn't mean lowering your standards—it means reclaiming your energy, your confidence, and your life.

JOURNALING EXERCISE

Dialing Back on Perfectionism

Perfection is an impossible standard that can weigh heavily on your energy, confidence, and joy. Today, explore what it might feel like to let go of the perfectionism burden . . . even a little.

1. **The Perfect Illusion:**

   - Where in your life or work do you feel the pressure to be perfect?
   - What does striving for perfection look like for you— in your thoughts, feelings, actions?

2. **The Hidden Cost:**

   - What has perfectionism cost you—in terms of time, energy, confidence, or peace?
   - What would you do with the time that the 80/20 rule could afford you?

3. **A New Belief:**

   - Reflect on the quotes by Albert Einstein and Vince Lombardi. Which words ring particularly true, and why?
   - What new meaning or insight could you take from the idea that "there's no such thing as perfect"— instead of only striving for excellence?

4. **Practicing Freedom:**

- What is one small step you can take this week to embrace "good enough"—to deliver something earlier, delegate more freely, or offer yourself more grace?

GENTLE REMINDER

Perfection is not the prize. Excellence, ease, and joy live in the space where enough is truly enough. Let go of the burden. You don't need the badge.

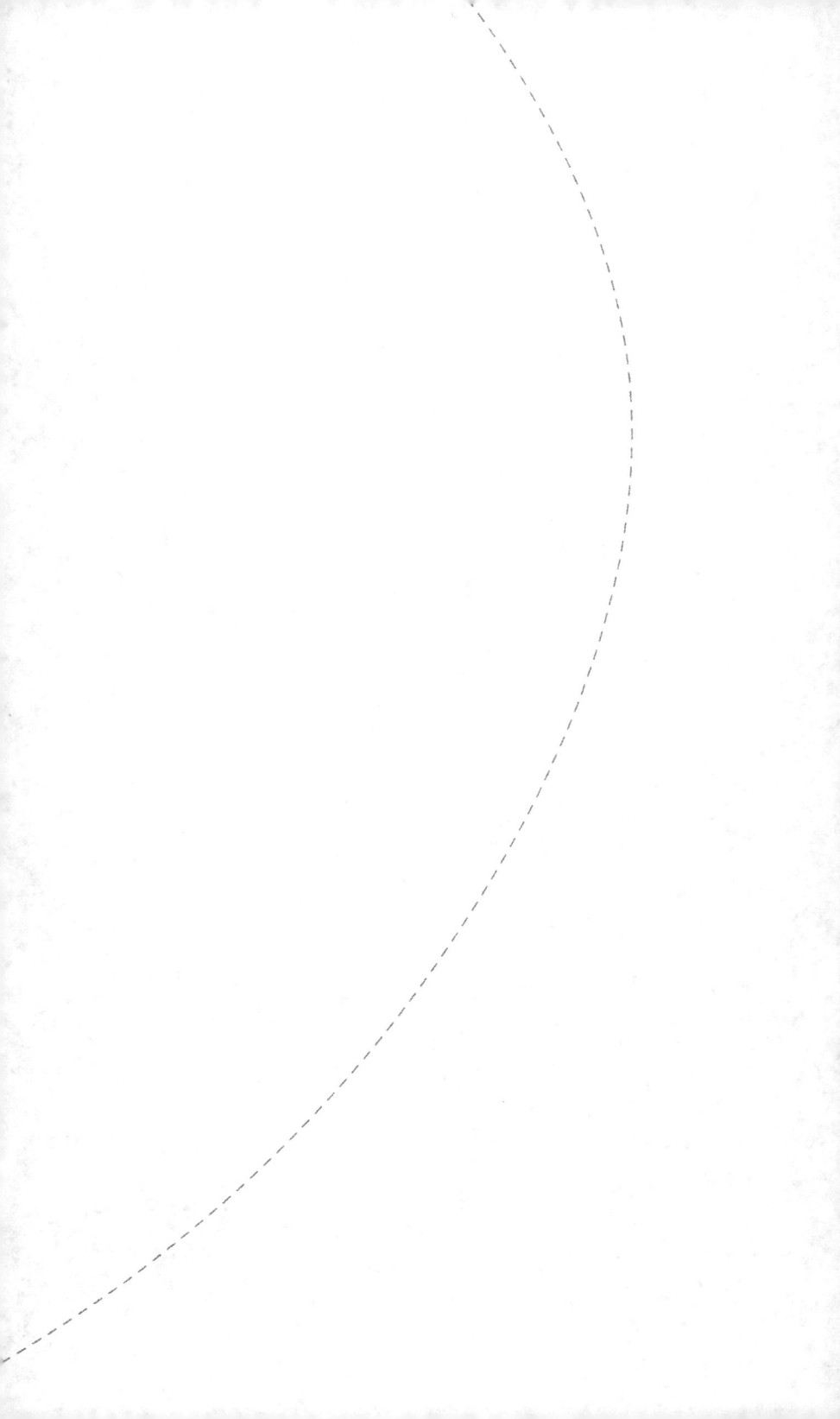

ARE YOU REALLY LISTENING?

IT STILL SURPRISES me how many of us believe we're great listeners—until we pause to actually examine *how* we listen.

During my coach training at Georgetown, I was introduced to the concept of listening as a skill, one that has levels. That got me thinking about my own habits. I had always thought of myself as a good listener. But was I really listening—or was I simply waiting for my turn to speak?

Years ago, I read a study that said we spend 70 to 80 percent of our waking hours engaged in communication. Of that time, 9 percent is spent writing, 16 percent reading, 30 percent speaking—and a whopping 45 percent is spent *listening*. And yet, most of us have never formally learned how to do it well.

We interrupt. We drift off. We rehearse our response before the other person even finishes their sentence. Sound familiar?

This came to life for me in my twenties when I noticed a pattern during family conversations. Someone would say, "I had an interesting day," and before they could finish, another person would jump in with, "You think *you* had an interesting day? Wait 'til you hear mine!" Within seconds, the conversation had pivoted—and not in the original speaker's favor. I began referring to this kind of interaction as **"What About Me?" Listening**—and believe me, once you notice it, you'll see it everywhere.

At Georgetown, I learned about three distinct levels of listening—each one deeper, richer, and more connected than the last. (The first level is even exactly what I used to call my family's conversation style!) We devoted a full class to this topic, and it was enlightening to gain this new insight. It was also extremely important because active listening is a core competency for becoming a certified coach. So, what's the difference between listening and active listening? Listening is simply hearing the words someone is saying. Active listening is leaning in with curiosity and care— paying attention to not just what's said but the feelings and intentions underneath, so the person knows they've really been heard.

***

Level One: "What About Me?" Listening

This is the level we fall into when we're distracted, rushed, or centered on ourselves. We sorta-kinda hear the other person's words, but we're really listening for the pause— the moment we can jump in with our story, our opinion, our advice. It's conversational ping-pong with no real rally. Harmless in small doses, but if this is your default mode, it can erode trust and connection over time.

Level Two: "All About You" Listening

This is where the magic begins. At this level, you're truly focused on the other person. You're listening not to respond but to understand. You let them finish their thought. You paraphrase to make sure you heard them right. You ask questions that show curiosity, not control. It's the kind of listening that makes people say, "Thank you for really hearing me."

Level Three: "All About Us" Listening

This is the deepest and most powerful kind of listening. At this level, you're not just hearing the words—you're picking up on the energy, the body language, the pauses, the emotion behind the message. You use your intuition. You create space for silence. You reflect back what you sense, not just what you hear. A Level-Three listener might say, "I'm sensing this project is really weighing on you— what's going on beneath the surface?" This level is where we're empathetic, attuned, and human. And when people experience this kind of listening, they don't just feel under-stood—they feel safe.

***

I've found that when I show up at Level Three, whether with clients, colleagues, friends, or family, something clicks. Conversations become more honest. Walls come down. Trust builds. And that's when the real connection begins.

We don't need to be perfect listeners all the time. But we do need to be intentional listeners. Because *being heard* is one of the most powerful gifts we can offer another human being.

JOURNALING EXERCISE
What Would Happen if I Listened More Intentionally?

Listening is more than hearing words. It's connection, under-standing, and being fully present. To some extent, it's about reading between the words. Reflect on how you listen—and how you might listen even more deeply in the future.

1. **My Listening Habits:**

   - When you're in conversations, do you find yourself listening to respond—or listening to understand?
   - What are some habits in yourself that you notice (interrupting, drifting attention, planning my reply)?

2. **Experiencing Deep Listening:**

   - Think of a time when someone listened to you so fully that you felt truly seen and heard. What made that experience so powerful?

3. **Leveling Up:**

   Ask yourself the following questions:

   - At which level of listening (One, Two, or Three) do I most often operate?
   - Which level would I like to practice more intentionally?
   - What is one simple action I can take this week to practice deeper, more intentional listening? (*Examples: letting silence happen without rushing to fill it, asking a clarifying open-ended question, noticing the speaker's emotions*)

GENTLE REMINDER

Listening isn't about waiting for your turn to speak—it's about offering someone your full presence. In a noisy world, be the one who listens well. It matters more than you think.

SAY IT LIKE YOU MEAN IT

I COACH A lot of smart, capable women—women who have bright minds, big ideas, and strong instincts. But there's one habit I see again and again that quietly chips away at their credibility. They ramble.

They'll make a great point . . . and then say it again . . . and again . . . circling the same idea with more and more words, hoping it will land even better the second or third time. But it doesn't. What actually happens is the message gets diluted, and the listener tunes out. This habit rears its head most often when they're speaking to senior leaders. They think more words will make them sound more prepared or convincing. But it simply isn't so.

One of the first pearls I share with my clients is this: **Say it once—with clarity and conviction.** When you do, you automatically sound more confident. You don't have to repeat yourself to be heard. You just have to be clear.

Sally, one of my coaching clients, embraced this shift beautifully. She was eager to grow and willing to experiment. In one of our sessions, we practiced getting a key message down to one strong sentence—and trusting that it was enough. She started trying out this technique in meetings. Before long, her manager told her she sounded more focused and effective. That positive, specific feedback boosted her confidence, and not surprisingly, she began getting invited into more strategic conversations with senior leadership.

And this isn't just something I teach—it's something I've had to practice myself.

When I was at Merck in my PMO leadership role, one of my responsibilities was to communicate the portfolio planning schedule for the upcoming year. I gave each of my direct reports the same PowerPoint slide to use when briefing their divisional IT areas. I was confident we had created a clear, consistent message, and I expected that by the end of the week, everyone would be aligned and ready to begin the heavy lifting.

Then I got a call from a divisional VP—and he was clearly frustrated. He told me that after hearing the update from my direct report, his team was more confused than ever. I was stunned. Everyone was using the same materials, and I hadn't heard any other concerns. In fact, most feedback so far had been positive. He asked if I would join a call the next day to walk through the plan with his leadership team myself. I agreed.

The next morning, I delivered the exact same content—same slide, same message—but with one key difference: I used clear, confident language. I did what I teach my clients: I saw the punctuation as I spoke (see below for examples). I used firm statements, not "maybes." I spoke as if the plan was already in motion—not still under construction.

When I finished, the VP responded immediately, "Thank you. Now we're clear." The message hadn't changed, but the delivery had. That's the power of clearly communicating. That's the power of presence.

So, let's take a deeper look into what I call, *See the punctuation when you speak.*

If there's a comma, pause briefly.

A period? Pause a little longer.

A question mark? Let your tone lift.

An exclamation point? Let your energy rise.

When you match your delivery to the natural rhythm of punctuation, your words become easier to follow—and more engaging. You begin to sound composed, thoughtful, and in control of your message.

Another topic that comes up when I'm coaching leaders on becoming more effective speakers is the *power of a metaphor*. Senior leaders are bombarded with information. A good metaphor cuts through the noise. It makes a complex idea stick. It paints a picture that listeners can instantly grasp—and remember. A well-placed metaphor isn't just clever; it's strategic. It elevates your leadership voice.

And finally, one of the simplest but most powerful communication tools I know: *The pause.*

A pause gives *you* a moment to think. It gives *your listeners* a moment to absorb. It's not empty space—it's intentional space. A well-placed pause can land your message more powerfully than a dozen extra words ever could. It signals presence. It signals confidence. In yet another way, it signals consideration for your listeners. *I'm going to give you a second to let that set in.*

When my clients begin practicing these tools—saying things once, seeing the punctuation for rhythm, adding metaphor, and embracing the pause—they don't just improve how they speak. They begin to show up differently. They are clearer and more compelling. They don't simply sound like leaders. They become them.

JOURNALING EXERCISE
Communicating with Clarity and Conviction

Think of a recent conversation in which you wanted to influence someone—especially someone more senior. How did you communicate your point? Did you repeat yourself?

- If you had the chance to say it again—with clarity and conviction—what would your one clear message be?
- What's one metaphor you could use to explain a complex idea you're currently working on? Take a moment to think about it.
- How do you feel about pausing when you speak? What would it take to become more comfortable with silence? What does it feel like when you hear people embrace the pause?

GENTLE REMINDER

You don't need more words to sound more credible. Say it once—clearly, confidently—and let it land. Fewer words can make it matter more.

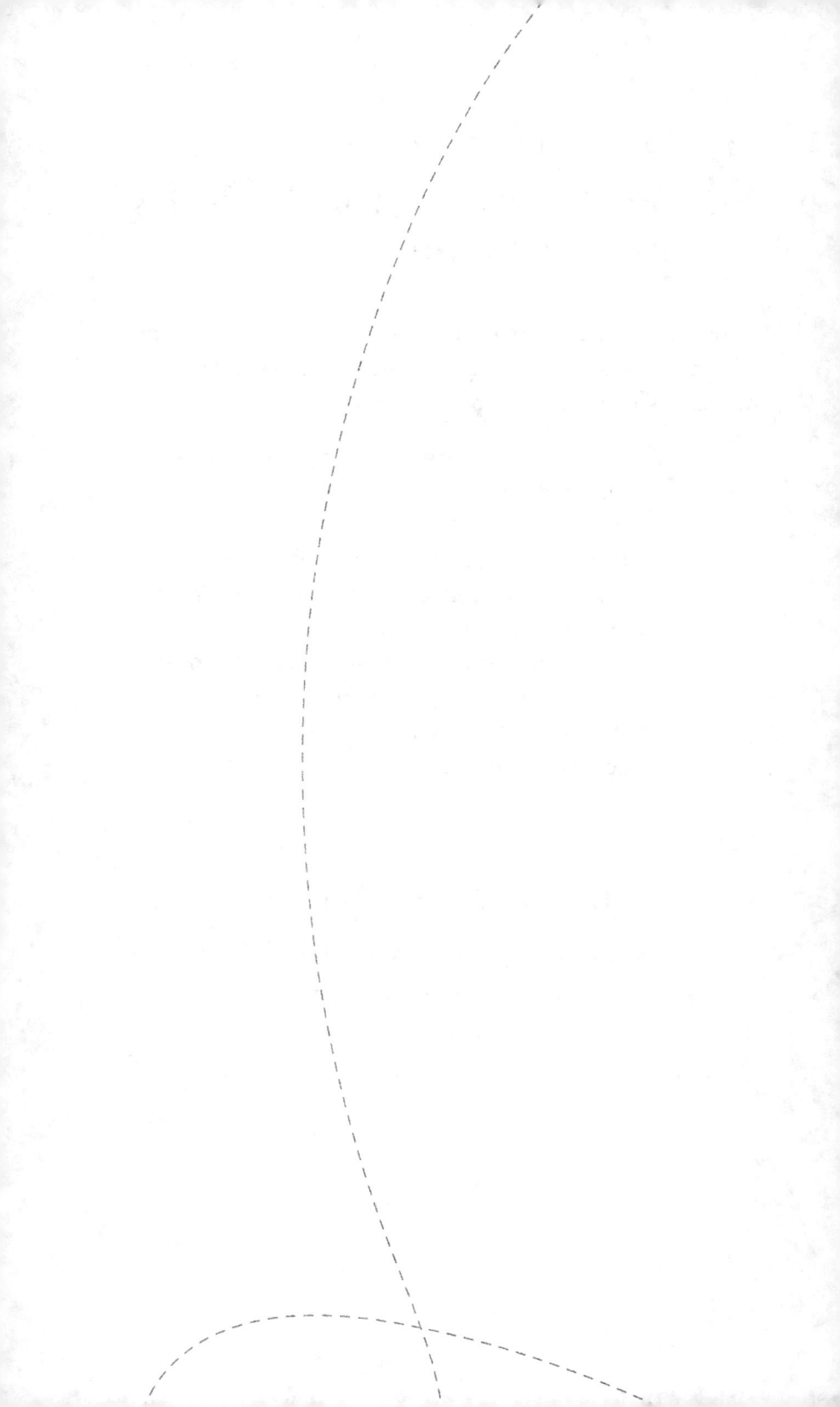

ACTIVATING MY SAGE

How Positive Intelligence Changed My Life

THE WORK *POSITIVE Intelligence* by Shirzad Chamine has transformed the way I show up every day of my life—as a human being and as a leader.

A year after I started my coaching business, one of my colleagues from my Georgetown leadership program reached out and asked if I'd like to join Shirzad's class, where he was training coaches on his research and teachings. I'd be in a pod with five of my Georgetown colleagues. I immediately said yes. I'd heard this work was powerful—a game changer for the coaching community.

With that backdrop, I enrolled in the multi-month program taught by Shirzad himself. We read *Positive Intelligence*, moved through the core modules, and practiced the tools each week in our pod.

The premise of the book is profound: We all have internal Saboteurs—negative voices that hijack our positive thoughts and emotions—and one Sage—our calm, wise, and resourceful inner voice. The goal is to quiet the Saboteurs and strengthen the Sage, allowing it to be more present.

What's brilliant about Shirzad's work is that he was the first researcher to clearly name and describe (with specific detail) the ten distinct Saboteurs that make up the negative voices in our heads. The master Saboteur for everyone is always the Judge, and each of us also has a unique combination of accomplice Saboteurs. Together the Saboteurs act as a "band of thieves," looking for every opportunity to rob us of our happiness, joy, and confidence. For me, besides having the Judge, my top two accomplice Saboteurs are the Pleaser and the Hyper-Rational.

The magic begins when you can notice and name the Saboteurs—because then you can begin to manage them. Over time, through the tools and daily practice, I became able to quiet my inner negative voice when needed and welcome my Sage.

Shirzad teaches how to activate the Sage through five powers:

- **Empathize:** Bringing compassion to yourself and others
- **Explore:** Engaging curiosity to understand what's really going on
- **Innovate:** Imagining new possibilities

- **Navigate:** Aligning with your deeper values
- **Activate:** Taking laser-focused, purposeful action

As a result of this work, I now live most days with my positive mind in charge. Of course, I still have negative moments, but they're far fewer. Recently, when I retook the StrengthsFinder assessment, *Positivity* showed up in my Top 10—at number 6—and it had never been a top strength before. That's a real shift.

I'm a coach who cares deeply about my clients, so this work has become one of my most treasured tools. When I graduated from Georgetown, my coaching declaration was to bring my heart and soul to my clients every day. Offering *Positive Intelligence* helps me live that intention. Many of my clients have embraced the framework as well and, as a result, have become noticeably happier and more confident. One client told me she now saves *ten* hours a week by no longer ruminating on negative thoughts. She uses that time to take her young daughter for walks in the park and reads books she never had time for before.

When I introduce Shirzad's work to clients, I love to share a visual I created to help me wrap my mind around the premise of his work with the intent of applying it more fully. Before practicing *Positive Intelligence*, I imagine I have a lavish, plush living room in my head—the kind you'd never want to leave. In the center are three oversized, ridiculously comfortable chairs—ones you sink into and can't get out of. Sitting in them: my Judge, my Pleaser

Saboteur, and my Hyper-Rational Saboteur. Every time I listen to their lies and the negative stories that they create, I picture myself spoon-feeding them the richest, most decadent chocolate cake with fudge frosting. If I do this, they aren't going anywhere. They will stay seated, growing fatter, more entrenched, harder to evict. They won't leave, and I certainly don't want that.

And I've also felt the power of activating my Sage. She's like having Wonder Woman in my mind—a force *not* to reckon with. She wears a light on her belt that shines like a lighthouse beacon. When she shows up—and these days, she's present most of the time—the Saboteurs scatter. Her light is so bright it has a blinding effect on the Saboteurs and strips them of their power. They flee from their chairs. And they don't come around too often anymore.

Let me be clear—I'm still human. Occasionally, my Saboteurs *do* show up. But now, I know what to do.

Last year, I was asked to be the keynote speaker at an Enterprise Architecture Summit. I said yes before I fully understood the scope: a one-hour presentation to five hundred people—incredibly smart people. And I'd never given a keynote before. After meeting with the sponsor (who assured me by saying she was thrilled to have me), I hung up the call and guess who showed up?

My Judge.

He told me I'd fail. That I'd be exposed as a fraud. That this would be the end of my coaching career. I was mortified—for ten long minutes. He went on and on with his negativity until I caught myself. I looked around and said, "JUDGE, you're fired. Out of here. There's no room for you in this process." I saw my Judge for what he was—a tired, old, decrepit man who was trying to steal my confidence when I needed it the most. I fed him no chocolate cake!

Then I called on my Sage and with her bright shining light I did a visualization exercise. I pictured every detail I needed for me to be an effective keynote speaker: the topic research I'd done, the hours I'd dedicated to talk preparation, my arrival at the event. I saw myself standing tall on stage, delivering my message with confidence, answering questions, and being applauded. I repeated that visualization often over the next three weeks.

And every time, I saw myself wearing a blue suit and silver shoes—neither of which I owned. So, the weekend before the event, I bought a blue suit and silver shoes. The keynote was a success, and I felt proud of what I accomplished. The next day, I received a beautiful bouquet of flowers from my daughter, Emma, with a card that read: *Congratulations Mommy on your keynote. You inspire me every day!* That card sits at the center of my workplace in my orange gratitude bowl, a collection of thank-you messages and encouragement notes gathered over the years from Emma and my clients.

Shirzad teaches us to turn negative thoughts into gifts and opportunities. And I do. Every morning, before I even get out of bed, I reflect on what I'm thankful for. It's a habit I now practice faithfully. I've learned that we get to choose how we want to live—happy or miserably. Because of the work I've done, my life is full—and I feel deeply grateful every day.

I choose happiness. Every single day.

JOURNALING EXERCISE

From Inner Critic to Inner Wisdom

You may not know their names, but you've likely heard the voices in your head. One pushes you to please, another over-thinks everything, and another tells you you're not enough. These are your inner critics, your Saboteurs. But you also have a wiser voice—your inner Sage—that is calm, clear, and deeply grounded. Let's explore.

1. **Looking Back:**

   - Think of a moment when your inner critic took over.
   - What did it sound like?
   - How did it affect what you did? Or didn't do?

2. **Checking In:**

   - When does that inner critic voice show up most often now?
   - Do you have more than one inner critic voice? If so, try naming it.
   - What situations tend to trigger it? Or them?
   - How do you usually respond?

3. **Looking Ahead:**

   - Think of an event or activity coming up at which you want to show up at your best.
   - If your Sage—your inner wisdom—were in charge, what would they say? What action would they help you take?

4. **Try This:**

- Tomorrow morning, before you get out of bed, name one thing you're grateful for. Let that small moment of intention set the tone for your day.

GENTLE REMINDER

We all have voices in our heads—some that lift us up and some that tear us down. The difference isn't whether they show up. The difference is whether we choose to feed them . . . or fire them.

PART VI

Continuing
the Journey

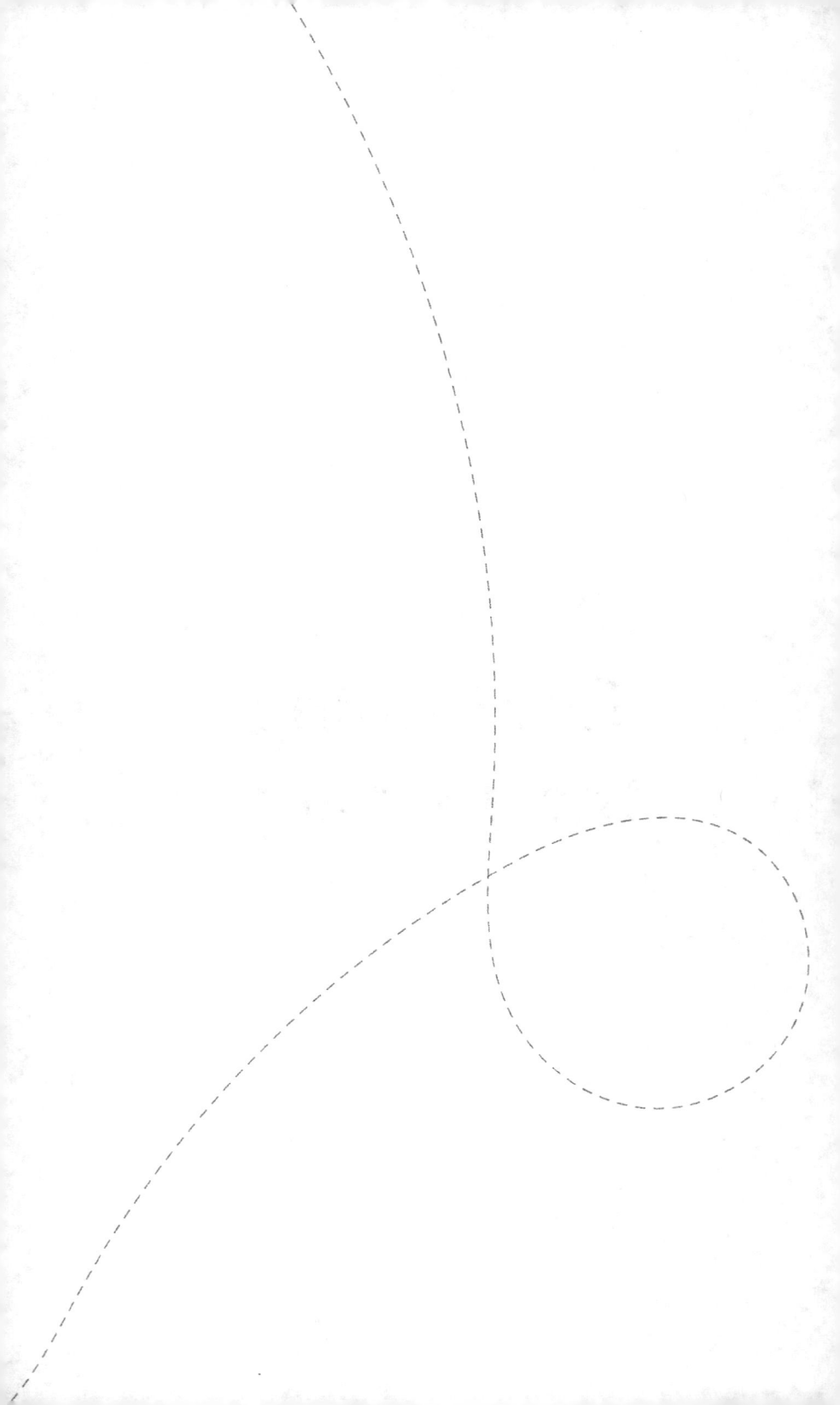

WHAT ARE YOU WAITING FOR?

MY CLIENTS ARE amazing, smart, creative, and capable people. But even among the most accomplished clients, I regularly hear something that always stops me in my tracks. They say they're *waiting*.

When a new job opens or a promotion is posted, they wait for their boss to recommend them. They wait for someone else to speak up. They wait to be noticed, to be invited, to be *ready*. So, I ask: **What are you waiting for?**

The word "wait" itself is just so passive. *To wait* is to delay action, to stay in place, to depend on something or someone else to move first. When I flip the question a bit and ask clients what they typically wait for, they smile and say things like: *an Uber, my flight, the doctor*. No one says, "I wait for permission to live the life I want." And yet, so many end up doing just that.

What I've learned is that this kind of waiting usually hides something deeper. Often, it's a lack of confidence or an inner voice (one of those Saboteurs!) whispering, *You're not ready. You're not enough. Not yet.* My clients want to feel 100 percent qualified before applying for the next-level job they've wanted for years. They want someone else to say they're worthy before they believe it for themselves.

But as I've shared in so many of the stories in this book—*clarity comes from action, not from waiting.* Growth comes from speaking up, not staying small. Leadership begins when you listen to your inner truth—and act on it.

I encourage my clients to manage their careers—and their lives—with intention.

To name what matters.

To speak their truth.

To stop deferring joy, purpose, or passion until the stars align.

Funny thing—coaching is never a one-way street. I'm grateful that my clients feel that they're learning from me, but the truth is, I've learned just as much from them. Their stories—and their courage—have pushed *me* to stop waiting, too.

After my divorce, I found myself stuck in a quiet pattern of hesitation. I wasn't doing the things I truly loved because I was waiting for someone to do them *with* me. Travel, dining out, chasing joy—I had tied these experiences to the presence of a partner. So, I waited. And waited. Until I didn't.

One New Years a few years ago, I booked a solo trip to Aruba. It was my gift to myself—a decision rooted in freedom. Sure, once I was there, there were moments when I felt alone. But I never felt lonely. I discovered that I genuinely love my own company. I challenged myself to try a new restaurant every evening. I talked with strangers. I people-watched. I savored food, cocktails, sunsets. I reconnected with the bold, adventurous part of me I had kept on pause. And I've kept the promise of not waiting.

Now I often dine out solo, and each time I do, I meet new people, try something new, or simply enjoy being me. My confidence as a solo traveler has grown—and so has my joy. This winter's "snowbird experiment" (my two and a half months in Florida enjoying sunshine over shoveling snow) is another chapter in this story. I didn't wait for a perfect partner, perfect timing, or a perfect plan. I simply asked myself: *What do I want?* I listened. And then—I acted.

That's the message I want to leave with you.

If you've made it this far in this book, you've done some important reflecting on your strengths, your story, your growth, and your possibilities.

So, I ask you now: *What are* you *waiting for?*

What part of your life have you put on pause?

What would change if you stopped waiting and started moving?

JOURNALING EXERCISE
Taking Wait Out of My Future

Sometimes we delay pursuing the things we most want—because we're waiting for the "right" moment, person, or permission. Today, give yourself permission to move forward. Consider the following as you do:

1. **Where Am I Waiting?**

   - What is one area of my life where I am "waiting" for something and putting off taking action? (Career, travel, relationships, personal growth, creativity?)

2. **The Story Behind the Waiting**

   - What story am I telling myself about why I have to wait?
   - Is that story really true?

3. **A Small Brave Step**

   - What is one small action I could take today—without waiting for anything or anyone?

4. **A Promise to Myself**

   - Complete this sentence: I will no longer wait for _____. I choose to _____ instead.

GENTLE REMINDER

You don't need permission to live the life you want. The pen is in your hand. The time is now. And you are ready.

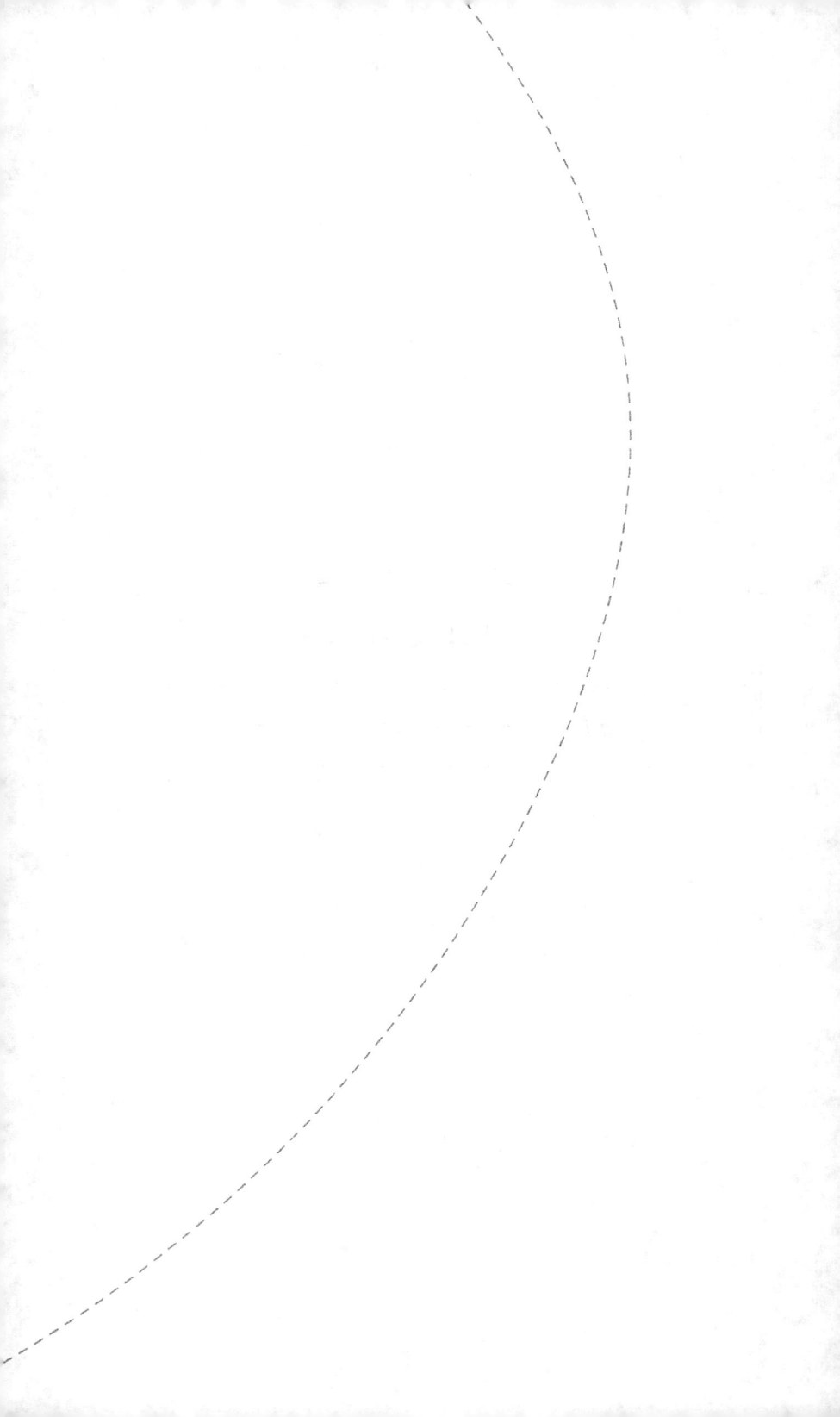

A NOTE FROM
ME TO YOU

WHEN I LOOK back on the stories I've shared—the moments of love, loss, courage, and growth—one truth becomes clear.

None of these experiences stood alone. Each was a thread—messy at times, luminous at others—woven into the larger fabric of who I've become. And if you're reading this, I believe the same is true for you.

This book is called *The Long Way Here* for a reason. It's about finding meaning in the moments, lessons in the challenges, and courage in the everyday choices that shape who we are. It's about recognizing that the steps you've taken—even the ones that felt uncertain—have brought you somewhere important.

Thank you for walking through these stories with me— for pausing to reflect, for honoring your own questions, and for opening your heart to possibility.

I didn't write this book to give you answers. I wrote it to remind you that you already have the wisdom within you. My hope is that something you read here stays with you—a sentence, a story, a question. Something that helps you feel just a little braver, a little more seen, and a little more ready to take your next step.

This book holds the voices of my clients, my mentors, my family, my younger self—and you. You are not alone on this journey. The questions you carry are the same ones many of us hold.

So, as you close this book, I hope you open something else—a new conversation, a new habit, a new dream, or a deeper connection to yourself. And if you're still wondering when to begin . . .

Start now. Start with what you have.

And trust that you're already on your path.

With deep gratitude,
Anne Spoldi

P.S.
LET'S STAY CONNECTED

IF SOMETHING IN this book spoke to you, I'd love to hear from you. Whether it's a reflection, a question, or a story of your own—I welcome it all.

You can find me at:

anne@partnerwithprossimo.com

or connect with me on LinkedIn at:

www.linkedin.com/in/annespoldi/

And stay tuned—my next book will be a companion to this one: a hands-on guide to the tools, frameworks, and coaching techniques I've shared with hundreds of clients over the years. If *The Long Way Here* helped you reflect, the next one will help you take action.

Until then, keep noticing the moments that matter.

Keep honoring your voice.

Keep connecting all the dots in your life that led you to where you are right now.

This isn't the end. It's just the beginning. Let's keep going—together.

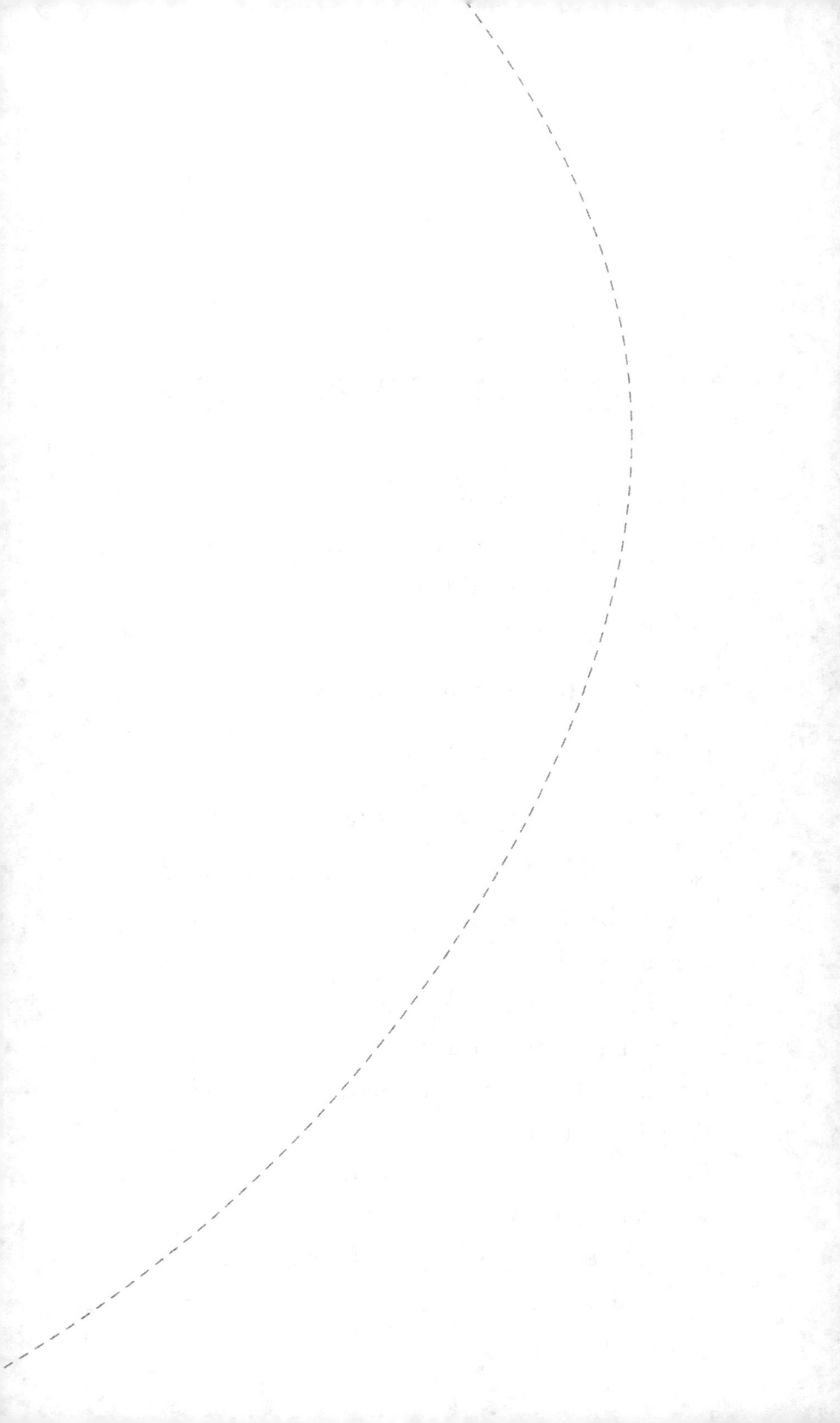

ACKNOWLEDGMENTS

As I reflect on my journey that brought this book into the world, my heart is full of gratitude.

To my beautiful daughter, Emma—you are my greatest inspiration. Your love, strength, and spirit have shaped me in ways beyond words. Every day, you remind me of what matters most.

To my family—thank you for your endless love, encouragement, and belief in me. You have been my foundation, my strength, and my greatest teachers throughout every chapter of my life. I carry you with me in everything I do.

To my coaching clients, I want to thank you for allowing me to walk beside you in your growth journeys. Your courage, curiosity, and commitment to becoming your best selves have been constant sources of inspiration for me.

To the gifted mentors, teachers, coaches, and friends who have encouraged me along the way—thank you for believing in me, for challenging me, and for reminding me that the dots would eventually connect.

To Kyle Rispoli, my personal trainer and friend. I often remind my clients that making time for physical exercise deserves to be scheduled ahead of everything else, because staying strong in body and spirit is a true priority. Thank you for helping me live that truth.

To my publishing team—Tracy Rothschild Lynch, my editor, and George B. Stevens, my book designer. I feel so blessed to have found you both. You have given me a wonderful lesson in what it takes to self-publish and made this process easy and collaborative. I deeply admire your professionalism and expertise, and value your encouragement along the way.

And to you, the reader—thank you for opening these pages, for trusting me with your time and attention, and for allowing these stories to become part of your journey too.

With deepest gratitude,

Anne

ABOUT THE AUTHOR

 ANNE SPOLDI has spent a lifetime navigating a winding road of leadership, reinvention, and human connection.

A chemist-turned-executive-turned-leadership coach, Anne brings decades of experience in science, technology, pharmaceuticals, and Fortune 500 firms—but it's her gift for seeing the person behind the title that sets her apart.

After beginning her career in a lab coat at GE, Anne followed a trail of curiosity and courage that led her from product management to Six Sigma mastery to executive coaching—with stops along the way at PerkinElmer, Sun Microsystems, and Merck. It was at Sun Microsystems, in the Executive Development Group where she reported to the Chief Learning Officer, that her passion for leadership coaching took root. Anne has since led global teams, managed multimillion-dollar change efforts, and worked closely with C-suite leaders to shape strategy and culture.

Through it all, one thing has remained constant: her belief that leadership is deeply human work.

Anne is the founder of Prossimo LLC, a coaching and leadership development practice grounded in empathy, candor, and real-world experience. *Prossimo* is the Italian word for *next*—and that's exactly what Anne helps her clients discover: what's next for them as leaders and human beings. A graduate of Georgetown's Executive Certificate in Leadership Coaching program and a Professional Certified Coach (PCC) with the International Coaching Federation, Anne helps leaders find their voice, trust their instincts, and grow into the people they were meant to be.

She wrote this book to share the stories behind the stories—moments of loss, love, doubt, clarity, and quiet courage that shaped her. She hopes you'll find pieces of yourself in these pages.

Anne lives in New Jersey and chases sunshine during the winters in warmer places. Her greatest accomplishment—and deepest joy—is being a mom to her daughter, Emma. She also loves cooking for friends, walking in nature, and starting her mornings with gratitude and strong coffee.

www.ingramcontent.com/pod-product-compliance
Lightning Source LLC
Chambersburg PA
CBHW060410130626
46555CB00005B/2016